$\mathcal{V}oices_{of}$
CONSEQUENCES
ENRICHMENT SERIES

Permission to Dream

12 Points to Discovering Your Life's Purpose
and Recapturing Your Dreams

By: Jamila T. Davis

Volume 2

VOICES
INTERNATIONAL PUBLICATIONS

Voices of Consequences Enrichment Series
Permission to Dream: 12 Points to Discovering Your Life's Purpose and Recapturing Your Dreams

This book is a nondenominational, faith-based instruction manual. It was created to inspire, uplift and encourage incarcerated women to overcome the dilemmas that led to their imprisonment and to provide instructions to help them discover their life's purpose and recapture their dreams. The author shares the strategies she has utilized, both spiritual and non-spiritual, to discover her talents and her purpose in life. This book is not written to promote any set of religious beliefs, although it does encourage readers to be open to receiving assistance from their "Higher Power" as they know Him.

The author of this book does not claim to have originated any techniques or principles shared in this book. She has simply formulated a system of proven strategies, from her research and experience during imprisonment, that her readers can utilize to discover their purpose and recapture their dreams. A comprehensive list of references used to create this work is located in the back of this book. Readers are encouraged to use this list to obtain additional books to further their learning experience.

Printed in the United States of America
First Printing, 2013

Library of Congress Control Number: 2012954501
ISBN: 978-09855807-4-2

Voices International Publications
196-03 Linden Blvd.
St. Albans, NY 11412
"Changing Lives One Page At A Time."
www.vocseries.com

Typesetting and Design by: Jana Rade, www.impactstudiosonline.com
Edited by: Kat Masurak and Theresa Squillacote

DEDICATION

This book is dedicated to every woman whose dreams have ever been shattered or stolen. I want you to know you can dream again and recover all that you have lost! You're not alone in this journey. Stay encouraged! This one is for you.

This book is also dedicated to four very powerful women, whom I met in federal prison, that helped to expand my imagination and stirred my faith: Dianne Wilkerson (a former state Senator), Ivy Woolf-Turk (a former real estate developer), Monnie Dorsey (a co-pastor and school founder), and Sujata Sachdeva (a former CFO of a fortune 500 company). Crossing paths with you all has changed my life. Thanks for your encouragement and inspiration. And, thanks for allowing me to learn from your experiences. You are living examples that life becomes great when you discover purpose. May this adversity lead to your greatest triumph. THINK BIG!!!

Permission To Dream

By Jamila T. Davis

Young lady, pick up your head and dry your teary eyes.
You don't have to stay stuck in a ditch; it's time for you to arise!
The past is done, so let it go.
A painful lesson, but now you know.
Everything that happened occurred for a reason.
The pain that you bear will only last for a season.
Never ever think it was all for nothing.
This storm has a rainbow; it will surely count for something!
It wasn't sent to hurt you or to even beat you down.
It's heaven's way of saying, "It's time to turn your life around."
Now that you're here, at this place, you're finally ready to soar!
Greatness lies just ahead, right behind the prison doors.
You're standing at the crossroads, divided by your choice;
You can take back what was stolen, by your imagination and
    your voice.
Revisit your days of youth, life as that little girl,
Who could become whatever she wanted or dreamed of in this
    world.
Take hold of all the dreams you had from way back then.
Embrace them like a treasure; treat them like your closest
    friend.
It's time to regroup, so that you can begin again.
Trust me; it won't be like before, this time you're sure to win!
Rise up and discard all the shame, regret and guilt.
On high self-esteem, this new house must be built.
You made some mistakes, but yet you're still a shining star!
Has anyone told you lately, how truly wonderful you are?

You're a special person. Yes, you're one of a kind!
God put you on this earth, for sure, to let your bright light shine!
Everything will come together, when you discover your purpose.
There's so much more to you than what appears upon the surface.
It's time to dig deep, and do some rearranging down inside.
It's time to show off your talents; you no longer have to hide.
Yesterday doesn't determine the state of your fate.
You can rise above adversity; it's never ever too late!
You can become whatever you desire;
And when you reach that goal, you still can go higher.
You no longer have to be afraid of what others think or what they say.
Young lady, it's your time to shine. Today marks a brand new day!
Give back all the baggage you've been given to hold you down.
Dust off your defilement; begin to turn your life around.
Stop regretting all the things you never got to do.
Instead do something about it, and experience something new!
Spread your wings and begin to fly!
Peel away your past, tell yesterday goodbye.
Yes, you can do it! Let your bright light beam!
Today I formally give you back your permission to dream.

My Acknowledgements

First, I would like to thank God; without You this project would not be possible!

Thank You for Your divine insight and revelations. May this book be used as an instrument to bring Your name praise, honor and glory.

I would like to thank my closest friend, my prayer partner and my business manager, Jeremiah Sills. You are absolutely incredible! Words cannot describe the respect and gratitude I have for you. You have been my legs and my arms! Your dedication and your passion have been an essential element in bringing this project to fruition. From the bottom of my heart, I truly love you!

To my mother, Liddie Davis, you are so amazing. Who would have ever thought our hardships would bring us so close together? Sorry for not recognizing sooner the extent of your unconditional love. I hope I have finally been able to make you proud.

To my dad, Hosea Davis, there are not many men built as strong as you. Your strength, love and encouragement have pushed me to levels I never could imagine I would accomplish. Thank you for your unconditional love and support.

Thank you Pastor Perry Mallory for believing in me and sticking by me on this journey. You will never be forgotten.

Thank you Kat Marusak for editing this book. You were truly sent to me by God, at the right time! Thanks for your hard work and dedication to this project.

Thank you Craig for always having my back. I will forever be your "ride or die" chick. Few know what loyalty is, but you surely know how to show it. Twenty years strong! I see you, baby. Let your light shine!

Thank you, Theresa Squillacote. In a dark place, I met a bright face. Thanks for fine-tuning all my projects. Your talents and skill-sets are recognized and greatly appreciated. You will forever be my Mozart.

To Meda, Talia, Quadree, Ivy, Loretta, Theresa, Shakila, Rose and Virginia, our friendship is for life! Friendships that are tested by the storms of life and still stand, these are the friendships that really count. I recognize each of you for your loyalty and your unconditional support.

To my brother Jules, thanks for your years of encouragement and support. You have no idea what you mean to me. I love you.

To Apostle John Testola, Prophet Wesley Van Johnson, Apostle Fannie Bowser and Bishop Itiola, thank you for giving me back my permission to dream.

To my children Kywuan and Diamond, may you reach heights I never could imagine. Thanks for being patient and loving me regardless of all my flaws. Always remember, come what may, Mommy loves you.

To Adelaide Gilmore, Rose Caban, Sakora Varone, Jamilah Smith, Keiha Laviscount, Roxanne Troy, Virginia Douglas, Loretta Fields, Tawanna Logan, Monique Johnson, Nicole Pfund, Theresa Marchese, Shakila Wallace, Desseray Wright, Natividad Santana, Riccia Goody, Maria Angelo, Edwina Bigesby, Monique Williams, Joylynn Grant, Andrea Goode-James, Gillian VandeCruize, Ingra Johnson-Barnwell, Rochina Brown, Laquan Lopez, Justine Moore, Sharon White, Phyllis Hardy, Rhonda Turpin, Renese Flowers, Denise McCreary, Vanee Sykes, Anne Lockwood, Stacey Goss, Christine Bursey, Linda Tribby, Theresa

Crepeau, Jane Beasley, Bethzaida Nazario, Gayle Phillip-Smith, Vanessa Valencia, Yajaira Navarro, Gwendolyn Hemphill, June Thousand, Lizette Morice, Alicia Maxwell, Carey Monteiro, Latesha Brown, and Rhonda Tigney, all whom I was imprisoned with at Danbury Federal Prison Camp, although I have known you all for a short period of time each one of you has touched my life in a special way. I am truly grateful to have met you. Thanks for holding me down. Stay positive, great things are just ahead!

TABLE OF CONTENTS

Introduction 1

Chapter 1 – The Power of Learning from the Past,
Then Letting it Go 7

Chapter 2 – The Power of Partnership with
a Higher Power 15

Chapter 3 – The Power of Positive Thinking 23

Chapter 4 – The Power of Recognizing Your Purpose 33

Chapter 5 – The Power of Developing Good Habits 43

Chapter 6 – The Power of Organized Planning 55

Chapter 7 – The Power of Desire and Faith 65

Chapter 8 – The Power of Specialized Knowledge Skills 75

Chapter 9 – The Power of Persistence and Focus 85

Chapter 10 – The Power of Love and Generosity 97

Chapter 11 – The Power of Enthusiasm and Balance 107

Chapter 12 – The Power of Perception 117

Afterword 127

INTRODUCTION

Permission to Dream

L ife consists of several cycles, good times, bad times, successes and failures. It is these cycles and spirals that make us aware of who we are and what we are made of. No matter what obstacles stand before or behind us, we are to recognize them as tunnels that lead us to discover the greatness that lies within. For many, this greatness or "other self" has been dormant, hidden within. It isn't until we run into our brick walls in life that we awaken to our true purpose. Realizing this purpose brings peace, happiness and joy. It fills the inner void that many of us mistakenly believed we could satisfy through external things. It is the true sense of accomplishment, honor and self-confidence, which we all have been longing for. Aware of the importance of this sense of purpose, many of us have chased false hope. Desperate for fulfillment, some of us have even sought the answer in drugs and alcohol. Regardless of how we sought relief, in the end we were deserted, disappointed and betrayed, left to begin again.

Many of us have fallen short of our dreams and goals. We have been beaten down by life's obstacles. We have been labeled unworthy or hopeless, leaving us defeated, with no clear direction of what to do or which way to go. Stuck behind prison bars, in a lonely cell, we have had to finally deal with the reality of our situation, knowing this is not the place we want to make our home. We've had nothing but time to repeat over and over in our minds all our mistakes, all of our flaws and the many bad choices that led us down this lonely path. Like a sharp knife stabbed in the middle of our hearts, we've had to accept the pain of our failure. Each day we wake up, constantly reminded of our circumstances by the closed doors we stand behind. Many of us have beaten ourselves up with shame and regret, unable to run, hide or forget our situation, which we were cleverly able to do in the free world. Prison has no place of escape. The walls are a constant reminder of our actions. This problem we cannot run from. This situation we will have to deal with. So let's make sense of it all.

We saw all the warning signs. We knew we shouldn't have been at that place at that time. Everything told us not to go, but we neglected to react to our inner voice and continued on the path we knew we shouldn't have gone down. "Only this last time," "I really need this money to pay the bills," and "They need me," were some of the excuses we told ourselves as we were lured into the wrong direction in life. Now that we are caught up in our situation, we get to see how clearly foolish our actions were. Many of us have been deserted by those very same people who promoted our behavior. We are left to realize, in the end, that real love would never have steered us in the wrong direction. Ashamed of our acts of foolishness, many of us have stay buried under sheets of hopelessness and depression. I've been sent to tell you, it's time to come out from under the sheets. Hard times won't last forever, but tough people do! We are built to last! We're going to make it! This is surely not the end; this too shall pass!

With every hardship, there comes equal opportunity for reward. It is up to each of us to identify the good or the opportunity that can come out of this adverse situation. Stop meditating on the bad. Let's explore the good.

For many of us, this is our first extended time of being still and silent. Life has been so hectic. We were constantly moving about and doing other things that many of us hadn't spent the time we needed to work on "self." Very few people in life ever master themselves, because of lack of time. This timeout can be a gift that most are not ever fortunate enough to receive. Imprisonment can be a blessing if you utilize your time wisely. It's time to start caring and working on "self." You are your biggest and most important asset.

Many of us were lost in life. We were so caught up into other people's lives and so many false illusions. This cycle has left us clueless. We don't even know our true "self." We have been in such a habit of pleasing others and doing what others like, that we haven't taken the time to analyze ourselves, what we like, where we want to be and what it will take to get there. It's time to get "self" together. It's time to analyze our defects, pinpoint our strengths and move forward successfully in life. When we master "self" we will quickly gain the keys we need to master life.

It is a common misconception that living life legitimately is hard or impossible for ex-convicts. "Nobody will ever hire me," "There's nothing else I can do," or "It's too late to change," are some of the popular excuses used by ex-felons. These statements are simply not true. You can be successful! You can be prosperous! You can make it! There is hope after prison.

This book will detail the steps you need to take to regain your dreams. Step- by -step we will walk together into discovering your purpose and the path to your success. Many others have walked in your shoes, and faced the same dilemmas you have. This book includes the success stories of women who overcame the obstacle of being an ex-felon. They made it, and you can too!

It's time to change your thinking. Many of our dreams were shattered a long time ago. Maybe it was your teacher who said,

"You will never make it." Maybe it was your mother whom you shared your dreams with, and she said, "You'll never be able to do that." Or, it might have been your closest friend who said, "You are not smart enough to achieve that goal." Whoever it may have been that counted you out and stole your dreams, they were wrong! You are smart! You do have potential! You can become whatever you want in life!

Today marks a brand new day. Yesterday is gone. It's today's choices that will determine your tomorrow. Your future is not in anyone's hands but your own. Today you can take back your power. Do you want to be successful? The choice is yours! You can achieve your goals, and this time you can do it legitimately!

Close your eyes and go back to your childhood days. Think about what you wanted to be when you grew up. Think about what you excel at. Picture yourself performing in your dream occupation. See yourself as successful. Picture yourself driving down the street in your dream car. Picture yourself parking your car and walking through the doors of your dream home. Feel the security of safety, knowing you don't have to look over your shoulder and behind your back. Walk though your home. See where your furniture is located; look at your family's pictures arranged on the wall. Isn't this vision wonderful? This can indeed become your life!

Today I formally give you back your permission to dream. Life isn't over. It just begun. Now it's up to you to take advantage of your opportunity to begin again. Take back all that has been stolen from you. Erase all the negative events that have robbed you of your hopes and dreams. Turn your pain into motivation to succeed. Roll up your sleeves, there's some work to do. First you must believe in yourself. Then, you can address your areas of deficiency and discover the techniques and practices of other successful people. They are no different from you and I. The only difference is their habits. If we want to be successful, we must develop successful habits.

Unlike the people of this world, success does not discriminate. It requires four main ingredients: belief, desire, passion and choice. Are you ready to travel down the road of success? If so, follow me.

This book will detail the steps you need to take to transition back into society. Not only will you become a law-abiding citizen, you will possess your dreams if you follow these proven formulas. Why not come out of prison on top? You don't have to settle for mediocrity! You can be great in the occupation of your choice. You are not alone. This time things will be different! Instead of moving through life aimlessly, you will come out with a plan and a road map to success. This time you will be prepared and ready for whatever comes your way.

You are a warrior. You've made it this far. Don't give up now! Dust yourself off from the defilement of your past. Don't remain trapped in yesterday. Yesterday is over. Let's get ready today for our tomorrow. Tomorrow the sun will come out. Tomorrow you will shine brightly. Tomorrow all your enemies will see what you are truly made of. Incarceration wasn't sent to kill you. It was sent to make you strong! Get your strength back. Put down your Kleenex tissue and embrace this book. The best is yet to come. Congratulations, your journey to success has officially begun. Your new life will prove to the world that dreams do come true!

Permission to Dream

CHAPTER 1

The Power of Learning from the Past, Then Letting it Go

L ife has dealt us many challenges. Unfortunately, many of us haven't taken the time to unveil the root of our problems. Until a problem is handled and uprooted it will continue to spread. Unhandled issues cause malfunctions in other areas of our lives.

Life is an obstacle course. There is a series of tests we have to go through, and we must pass them. With each test we pass, we then advance to the next level or the next cycle of life. If we don't pass our test, we have to repeat the course. Many of us have consistently flunked the same test, which causes us to have to face the same obstacles. The only differences are the new people and places we encounter. Until we get this thing right, we will remain stuck. Only an insane person does the same things and expects different results, but many of us have earned our title of "insane." It's time to take hold of life and defeat our negative cycles.

Many of us have been bruised and defiled by shame and guilt. These two emotions can be deadly if you wallow in them. They undermine self-esteem and motivation, keeping you trapped in a nonproductive mode.

Shame is an emotion that we feel when we do something that disappoints the people we love or admire. When we are shameful we are vulnerable to being controlled by others. Shame can affect each choice we make and prevent us from recognizing good opportunities. Shame ignites the false belief that we don't deserve the best. When we remain stagnant in shame we are locked in our own inner prison called low self-esteem.

Guilt is believing that what we did wasn't okay. This can be good when it signals us to correct our unethical behavior. Guilt is resolvable. We resolve guilt by acknowledging our adverse behavior and changing our conduct. Shame isn't easily resolvable. Shame leaves us with the feeling that we are inadequate and that there is nothing we can do to fix it. Shame leaves us hopeless, and provides no solution.

Today we must release our feelings of shame and guilt. We do this by changing our conduct and making amends with our past. What happened in the past cannot be taken back. We must forgive ourselves and accept responsibility for our future. We can move forward in life with precision. Our past does not have to determine our future. It is up to each of us to do the necessary work within to guarantee success for tomorrow.

Let's learn from our mistakes. What has this experience taught you? What can you do that you haven't done in the past that will make your future successful? What will you chose to change? What bad choices will you vow to never make again? When you embed these answers in your mind and apply them to your life, you will have adopted a system that allows you to learn from your mistakes. Some of the most valuable lessons in life come from experience. Because of what you have gone through, you will not make the same mistakes that others will fall prey to. Life has taught you many valuable lessons: What and what not to do, where and where not to go, and most importantly, who and who not to associate with. Keep these lessons, but throw away the bones! Don't hold onto the resentment, guilt or shame from your past.

Life is filled with many grand opportunities for us to take hold of. The trick is we must recognize those hidden opportunities that come in the form of misfortune or temporary defeat. This is the reason why many people have failed to seize opportunities that come across their path. Before anyone achieves success they must meet failure or temporary defeat. It is our failures that train us and prepare us for lasting success. Most people are not aware of this truth, so they allow failure to take them out of the game, and they quit. Failure has a way of tripping us up or delaying us when success is just ahead, within our reach. It is our job to learn how to profit from life's lessons, both good and bad. We do this by analyzing the lessons taught in them. When we learn from these lessons, we are able to convert defeat into stepping stones to success. It is time that we accept our past and use it to propel us into the future. We do this by changing our thinking. We must perceive ourselves as successful. Success comes to those who are success-conscious. It's time for us to take on a winning attitude, keep our eyes on the prize and persevere towards our goals.

It's important that you really understand the true meaning of success. Success is not just having a good career and money. True success is wholeness in every aspect of our lives - in mind, body and soul. Success is being happy and stable in our emotions, relationships, business, finances and our health. It is the complete package. Success as people often measure by the world's standards isn't always true success. People may have one area covered, yet they lack in another, and that one missing piece can ruin the entire picture. It should be our goal to obtain true prosperity, nothing missing and nothing broken. The *Voices of Consequences Enrichment Series* will give you the steps needed to achieve complete wholeness. This volume of our series will deal with the areas of success in family, business and finances. This book will give you the tools you need to obtain your goals and to be prosperous.

It is not good enough just to work hard, you must work smart. Working smart requires wisdom. In order to obtain success you must learn the principles successful people use. Successful people have successful habits. Many of them have dealt with the same dilemmas we face; the difference is they confronted them head-on and conquered them. Successful people are courageous. They believe in themselves, and they believe in their dreams. They are passionate about their success, and they refuse to allow anyone to get in the way of pursuing their dreams. Success is a choice that becomes a lifestyle. Those who excel in life follow the principles of successful living. Adversity will never destroy the person who has courage and faith.

We now stand in the chambers of adversity. At times it can be painful, but adversity has many benefits. It is the place where we can weigh on the scales of life those who profess to be our friends. It is also the home of awakening to "self." In the fiery furnace, we learn who we are and what we are made of. We discover our gifts and talents as well as our weaknesses. Trials are God's way of developing us and forcing us to become strong. God is not depriving you; He is setting you up for your greatest victory! How can you be a warrior if you don't know how to fight? How can you retain riches if you don't know what to do with them? Everyone in life is tested and tried. Each of us grows in steps and stages. Adversity is our launching pad to success. Therefore, this obstacle was necessary. It will propel us into who we are destined to become—great people! When we accept life's challenges and embrace them, we are able to receive the intended lesson. Then, we can move forward.

Just as a baby who is learning to walk gets up, takes a step and falls down, then gets up again and eventually begins to walk, we will now rise up and soar. Nothing else matters except for today. Today we are brand new creatures. We were blessed to see another day, and we are able to walk in strength. Be grateful.

Take a moment and think of all you have to be grateful for. What do you have that many others do not have? How has God blessed you? Ponder these thoughts and write the answers in your journal. When times are rough, begin to think of all the gifts you have and for which you are grateful. This perspective will begin to shed light on who you truly are, even in the midst of your adverse circumstances.

At the end of each day, take time out to mediate. Go over the events of the day. Analyze what lessons you have learned, and make a mental note of what you would like to correct. Then, envision your day going the way you wanted it to go with your corrections applied.

We become better in life through practice. Practice must occur on a consistent basis. Therefore, we must set goals and work hard to obtain them. Staying focused and prioritizing what's important is essential for success. Don't dwell on what you have no control over. Dwell on what you can indeed change.

Now it's officially time to say goodbye to yesterday. Gather all your nuggets of wisdom and the lessons you have learned, and store them in your mind. Picture your past being thrown into a capsule. Stuff as much sorrow and unhappiness into it as you can, and seal it. Go down to the river and throw the capsule as far away into the water as you can. It's done, it's finished, and it's over!

Say this affirmation with me: *"Today marks my new beginning. Today is the day I decided to begin again. Yesterday is over. I will not allow it to hold me down ever again. I will no longer feel ashamed or guilty because of my past. Today I have forgiven myself and others who have wronged me. I accept my past failures and I recognize them for what they truly are. They are my launching pads to success. My life experiences have equipped me with the wisdom and knowledge necessary*

11

to prevent me from making the same mistakes again. I have learned my lesson, now I will move forward vigorously!

My mind is centered on success. I love myself, and I believe in myself. I can become whatever I put my mind to. I am focused, and my mind is clear. I will no longer allow distractions to come in the way of my success.

I look at this time of imprisonment as my gift to work on my greatest asset, which is "self." I will work diligently to do all I can to improve myself. I will hurdle over this obstacle of imprisonment. It will no longer hold me down; it will only make me a stronger, better person.

Today, I have opened my eyes. I see life for what it really is. Today I have discovered my opportunity to become a greater being. I accept this opportunity and the challenge that comes with it! I am determined to make the best out of my situation."

Now let us say a short prayer: *"God, give me strength to surrender to You those things I cannot solve. Open my eyes to see life from Your perspective. Expose me to my gifts and talents, and lead me into Your perfect purpose for my life. Help me to deal with the pain of my past and to discard it. Help me to become whole again, nothing missing and nothing broken. I now receive Your divine hand of intervention and protection, all the days of my life. Amen."*

CHAPTER QUESTIONS

1) Write down a list of what you've learned from your past failures.
2) What steps will you need to take to prevent future mistakes in these same areas?
3) What are you truly grateful for?
4) How can you use your time of imprisonment wisely?

5) Why is failure at times necessary to obtain success?

WRITING ASSIGNMENT

Write your own affirmation of success. Detail what you want to accomplish and the steps it will require. List the main goals you wish to achieve in the next five years. State them as facts (i.e. I will spend my time in prison studying how to become a better me. Upon my release I will go back to college. I will study hard and obtain good grades).

CHAPTER 2

The Power of Partnership with a Higher Power

Regardless of the pain, hardships and spirals of life, it is important to understand we are not alone. One of the common mistakes of mankind when experiencing trials and tribulations is to detach, and blame God. The common theory is, "If God loved me, He would have never let this happen," or "God is supposed to be good, but a good god would have never let this happen to me." These theories develop into hate and resentment of our Higher Power, causing us to detach from the very Source we so desperately need. This approach leaves us helpless and vulnerable to the deceptions of evil.

God's thoughts are not like our thoughts. His ways are higher than our ways. Unlike us, He knows the beginning, middle and the end. There is always a reason "why" He allows things to happen the way they do. It is not our job to figure out or to understand totally God's plan. It is our job to surrender, which means to accept God's will, whatever it may be. We surrender, knowing all things will work together for our benefit.

Imprisonment is a good time to develop a relationship with our Higher Power. Many of us know of the concept of a Higher Power from our parents, friends or even a spiritual advisor, but there is a big difference between knowing of God and having a relationship with Him. A relationship with God is built on trust and intimacy. When we get to know God, His character and His ways, the door of our hearts open, enabling us to trust Him. When we learn to trust God, we no longer murmur and complain about circumstances we are unable to control. Instead, we begin to trust that God has a reason for allowing certain obstacles to exist. We know, no matter how bad things may seem, everything will work together for our good. All suffering bears an opportunity for an equal reward.

Intimacy is establishing a relationship. Just as there is a difference between a relationship with an acquaintance and your husband, there is a difference in knowing of God and knowing God intimately. When we spend time studying God's Word, learning His ways and applying these attributes to our lives, we become intimate with God. Intimacy does not happen overnight. Like any relationship, it must be developed over time. Each day that we take time to spend alone in meditation, in prayer and in reading the Word of God, we develop a stronger relationship with God that leads to intimacy. Intimacy has its advantages. It comes with the reward of faith.

Faith gives us the strength and ability to endure whatever obstacles may come our way. When we develop faith, we are no longer shaken by obstacles. When obstacles appear that are too strong or heavy for us to bear, we can hand them over to God and receive the faith we need to carry on. Our relationship with God rewards us with peace of mind and rids us of fear, worry and doubt. We have peace because we have an assurance, through our intimacy, that God will handle every problem that we can't handle. We know if there is an action we must take, He will lead us and guide us in the way we should go. Knowing this, we have peace when others who lack this relationship are troubled and overburdened.

As we journey through life endeavoring to "begin again," we need assurance or a guarantee that we will be led and guided not to make the same mistakes we made before. We can gain this assurance by making our "Higher Power" our Partner. He desires to help us, but we must invite Him into our lives through prayer. Through prayer we surrender our will over to our new Partner, God. We ask Him to lead us, guide us and direct us. We also ask Him to fulfill our desires, but we ask that it be done only if it is God's will. We learn God's will through His Word. Whatever God's Word states is a promise and an assurance that belongs to us.

Unfortunately, too many of us don't know all the wonderful promises of peace and blessings that God offers us, so we never redeem them. That's the equivalent to a bum living on the streets and eating out of a garbage can, unaware that his uncle has died and left him millions of dollars in his will. If the bum never claims his inheritance, he will die a pauper and suffer the anguish of poverty when he could have lived a very pleasant, wealthy lifestyle. This analogy represents many of us who have been living contrary to how we could be living. Many of us suffer because of lack of knowledge. It's time for us to gain wisdom and knowledge so we know what to do and how to do it. It is the awakening of wisdom and knowledge that will lead us into true success. The beginning of wisdom starts by studying God's Word and developing an intimate relationship with Him.

It's easy to push forward when we know that we are not alone. When we understand that, no matter where we are or what we do, God is with us, we have the faith and courage we need to persevere and overcome any obstacle we may encounter. Whenever we become weary, we know we can take a time out, get quiet and seek the assistance of our Partner, God. He will lead us and guide us into the truth of what we should and should not do.

The theory of prayer seems senseless to many people. They believe they are speaking to someone or something that can't or won't answer them. This is because these people are not "in tune" with their Higher Power. When seeking communion with God, we must learn how to approach Him and how to listen for His voice. Mastery of these techniques comes with time and experience.

Prayer is speaking to God and voicing our desires. We can do this in any place-at work, at home, in the grocery store, and even in prison. Whenever we find ourselves needing our Partner, we should seek Him simply by speaking to Him as you would speak to your best friend. He is always there; He hears you and desires to help you. You must know this! When you invite God to be your Guide, He stands up to accept the assignment. As He becomes your Friend and your Partner, make it a practice to call upon Him, not only during trials and tribulations, but also during the good times. Develop a habit of thanking God for all that He has done and is doing. God loves an attitude of gratitude. When we begin to thank God for what He Has already done, He delights in giving us more. Giving God thanks also strengthens us. It takes our mind off what we don't have and makes us grateful for what we do have. This sense of gratitude sparks joy deep down within us, giving us the strength we need to move forward with excellence.

Meditation is the way we receive answers to our prayers. Often we are too busy talking and moving about, unable to receive the answers to our prayers. God is serene. He speaks in a soft, still voice. You cannot hear the voice of God when your mind is too busy. In order to hear from God we must clear our minds and become still. We are to concentrate our thoughts solely on God and His goodness. We are to commune with Him through our minds, with a desire to hear from Him. When we are still, He speaks by dropping subtle thoughts into our spirit, which translates to our minds. He gives us peace through revelation. It

18

may be that the one idea which you forgot about that He reveals to you through meditation. Be still and learn to hear God's voice. He's been talking to you, but have you been listening? When you are in need of God's help, be still, quiet your mind and open your heart to listen.

I was blessed to discover an excellent method of prayer that I will share with you from Norman Vincent Peale's, *Power of Positive Thinking*. This formula has helped me develop a more intimate relationship with God; I pray it will do the same for you.

Norman Vincent Peale's formula of prayer is: (1) Prayerize, (2) Picturize, and (3) Actualize. Prayerize means to create a daily system of creative prayer. When problems arise, talk them over with God on a simple, intimate basis. View God as a Partner or a "Close Associate." Make prayer a continuous action. Pray as you walk, talk and move through the day. Know God is always with you, no matter where you are.

To picture is to see what you ask for as already being done. The man who assumes success tends already to have it. To assure something will happen, first pray about it and check it out according to God's will, which is His Word; then print a picture of it in your mind as happening. Hold that picture firmly in your mind. See it and feel that it is done. Feel the emotions that come with this experience as if you already have it. Continue to surrender that picture daily to God's will. Then, put the matter in God's hands and follow His guidance. It is essential that you do your part in achieving your desire. Always remember, faith without works is void. It is our job to work with God. He is our Partner. Practice believing and continue picturizing your desires in your thoughts until they come to pass. You will be amazed at the mysterious ways in which picturization materializes.

To actualize is to experience the answer to your prayer. After we prayerize and picturize what we desire, God will actualize it. It will come to pass! It is God's power that actualizes our prayers. As we partner with God in prayer, our prayers become our reality!

We now have the information we need to develop the most successful partnership any human can have. Wouldn't it be good to have a Partner Who is all-knowing, Who has all the answers to life, and Who holds all the power of the world in His hands? Well, invite Him into partnership with you today. Let's do it together: *"God, I know that without You I can do nothing. I realize in my own strength, the problems I endure I cannot overcome. But with Your assistance, I know that all things are possible. Therefore, I invite You into my life to be my Partner and my Friend. Lead me and guide me to the way in which I should go. Open my heart, and help me clear my mind so I can hear Your voice of direction. Teach me how to develop an intimate relationship with You. Answer my prayers when I call upon You. Allow me to feel Your presence of love and compassion. I mark today as my new beginning with You. Today You are no longer just my God, You are my Partner and my Friend. Amen."*

Now that you have invited God in to become your Partner, you have opened the doors to everlasting help and strength. You now have the power to endure any problem, circumstance or situation. Whenever you are troubled, you can call on your Friend. Wow, what greater assurance can you have than that to succeed in life? Congratulations, victory is just ahead.

Let's close this chapter with an affirmation that you can say daily to remind you of this new partnership you have: *"Today I will succeed. Today I will overcome. I have this assurance because God is my Partner. If trouble comes my way, today I won't fear. If evil comes in my direction, today I have no need to run. I will stand strong and call on my Partner. He will help me. He will deliver me. Because I have Him, I can do all things. Nothing is ever too difficult for my Partner to resolve. What was hard for me yesterday, I can do today with ease. What bothered me or overwhelmed me yesterday, I can quickly dismantle and overcome today. My victory is obtained because my Partner is greater and bigger than any obstacle. Having this assurance, today I shall overcome! Amen."*

CHAPTER QUESTIONS

1) Why is partnership with God necessary in life?
2) What is prayer?
3) What is meditation?
4) What is the difference between knowing of God and having a true intimate relationship with Him?
5) Describe the steps to Vincent Peale's prayer formula in your own words.

WRITING ASSIGNMENT

Write down your own prayer agreement with God as your new Partner. Tell Him what He means to you. Thank Him for the things you are grateful for. Tell Him what you expect to experience in your new partnership with Him. Keep a record of what you are praying for, and visualize your prayers being answered. You will be amazed as you go back to your records and see how God faithfully answers your prayers that line up with His will.

CHAPTER 3

The Power of Positive Thinking

In our journey to liberation, it's important to understand the power of the mind. The mind is the central station of the body. It is the place that gives the commands to which the body reacts. Wholeness is derived from the disciplined mind. When our minds are in harmony with our Higher Power, we begin to experience peace and serenity. Therefore, our greatest mission is to discipline our minds and to conquer our thinking.

Our character, which represents who we truly are, is a sum total of all our thoughts. Every act that we commit is a result of our thoughts. We have to think in order to perform. In essence, our thoughts become reality; they are materialized by our actions. We are what we think. So the question is, what have you been thinking about? Examine yourself and your current life. These factors reveal the content of your thoughts.

In order to change our lives, we must change our thinking. It must be our goal to elevate our minds with positive thoughts. We accomplish our mission by controlling our thinking patterns. We cannot allow negative thoughts to take root in our minds. Wrong thinking creates bad habits, which then materialize into a negative lifestyle. If this pattern continues and is not corrected, it ultimately leads to self-destruction.

Our universe is governed by laws. Many of us are familiar with the law of gravity. We are able to stand up straight and not fall because of this law. Universal laws cannot be negated. The law of attraction is another universal law. It states "like attracts like." Our thoughts create energy that propels into the universe: Whatever we focus our thoughts on attracts like energy to us. For example, if we are in constant fear of something, the energy of fear we create will dispatch more fearful energy towards us from the universe. Therefore, our thoughts materialize into our reality. For many of us, this has been the root of our problems. We have focused on negative things for so long that our lives now exhibit the fruit of our thoughts—disaster!

There is only one way to achieve wholeness. Wholeness begins in the mind. We must train our minds to become positive. We do this by feeding our minds with positive thoughts. We are able to monitor our thoughts by monitoring our emotions. Our emotions signal us to the state of our thinking. If we are feeling sad or depressed, it is because sad or depressing thoughts are flowing through our minds. When we change our thoughts, our emotions will automatically change. This reveals to us the secret to happiness. Happiness is established from within. If you want to be happy, concentrate on happy thoughts. Visualize yourself as happy. Picture yourself achieving your dreams. These thoughts will generate peaceful, happy emotions. They will also signal the universe to bring more happy energy your way. Eventually, if you practice maintaining these positive thoughts, they will become your reality.

Each day as you awaken, take control over your day by setting your mind on what you want to experience. Before you get out of bed, establish in your mind that your day will be good. Visualize yourself accomplishing the tasks you need to perform successfully. When you visualize your day, it is important that you "feel" the positive emotions you are thinking. Purposely, feel at peace. Feel happy. Feel joy coming from deep within your soul.

Think about what will make you happy. When you do this, you send signals to your mind that create positive energy, which is dispersed into the atmosphere. This energy is the roll call that picks up other energy in its likeness and brings it to you.

How we start our day is very important. It sets the tone for the rest of the events to come. Think about days when you woke up to a disaster. The kitchen floor flooded, your car wouldn't start or you missed the bus. Then, think about the events that spiraled downward after that. Everything seemed to go wrong, why? Because you thought in your mind you would have a bad day, and that thought brought further bad experiences.

Whenever you experience difficulties, take a time out. Go to the bathroom or a quiet place and empty out your mind. Meditate and purposely root out all negative thoughts. If you're angry, force yourself to be at peace. If you're afraid, encourage yourself to have faith. If you're nervous, anxious or worried, release those thoughts. Tell yourself: "All is well, everything is going to be okay. Today is a good day. I will rejoice and be glad in it." You can further enhance your feelings by recounting all that you are grateful for. Begin verbally giving God thanks. Thank God for allowing you to see another day. You will be amazed how performing this small task can eliminate all negative thoughts and allow you to see the good in your day.

Always remember, life is whatever you see it as or label it as. If you call the day good and look for the good with expectancy, you will experience the joy of the day. If you believe your day is going to be bad, you will attract your belief, causing your day to be miserable. Knowing this, we must force ourselves to look for the good in every situation, then express gratitude. The emotion of gratitude is one of the most powerful emotions we can experience. It signals to the universe that you are grateful. Then, the universe in turn rewards you with more good things because of your gratitude. No matter what you go through in life or how little you feel you have, take the time out to give God thanks for what you do have. You'll be sure to receive more. Live life with an attitude of gratitude.

In order to keep our minds at peace, we must guard the energy we allow into our inner circle. Thoughts are contagious. If we associate ourselves with negative people, we have a strong potential to pick up their negative thinking patterns. Have you ever been in a really good mood and then spent time with a person who is sad and complains about all their problems? Then, by the end of the conversation, do you feel drained, depressed and defeated too? Of course; because that person contaminated you with their negative thoughts. Never allow anyone to dump their trash in your can! Don't entertain negative conversations. Take the lead. Look for the good in the situation and highlight it in your conversations. If the conversation still doesn't become positive, opt to leave. By doing this you maintain your good mood and your focus.

It is important that we evaluate the company we keep. If a person doesn't uplift and encourage you and your purpose in life, don't spend time with them. Surround yourself with positive people and watch how their positive energy will inspire you. As you change your mindset and set good goals, you will attract new positive people into your inner circle. These people will enhance your life and keep you planted on the right track.

Now that we have talked about the function of our thoughts, let's explore the subconscious mind. The subconscious is the part of the brain that picks up the impulses of thought and emotions and records them. It is the "sending station" of the brain, through which vibrations of thought are broadcast into the universe. We can voluntarily plant seeds of thought into the subconscious mind. Our subconscious acts on the dominating desires we have that are mixed with emotions and feelings of faith. We cannot entirely control our subconscious mind, but we can voluntarily inject our plans, desires and purpose into it through thought. As we absorb these thoughts, the subconscious transmit them into the universe. Then, our desires are manifested in our reality.

It is the subconscious alone that is the medium through which prayer is transmitted to our Higher Power. Prayer is essentially our desire. As we meditate on our desires, we are asking God to bring these things into our path. Just as we are careful about what we ask for in prayer, we should be just as careful of the thoughts we allow to fill our minds.

God communicates with us through thought. As we pray and meditate, He sends us answers back through our spirit, which translates to our thoughts. Have you ever been going somewhere and a thought drops into your mind out of nowhere that advises you to go in another direction and you obey, to later find out something terrible happened in the direction you were going? That was God speaking to you through thought. How about before you were arrested, did you have a thought that said, "Don't go there today, tell them no?" That was also God communicating with you through thought. It is imperative that we come into consciousness with "self" and learn to listen for the voice of God.

Just as God communicates with us through thought, so does the enemy of our souls. Idle minds are his workshop. He constantly sends negative messages to our minds. He torments us with thoughts of fear, worry, doubt and other negative ideas. If we accept those thoughts as our own and concentrate on them, we help bring that negative energy into reality in our lives. Don't sign for the package! Reject negative thoughts! When they come to you, negate them by thinking positive thoughts. A good way of doing this is to practice using positive affirmations. They will help cancel out all negative thoughts that come your way.

It is our job to feed the mind. If we leave it idle, negative weeds will sprout up. A good way to feed the mind with positive thoughts is to read and meditate on scriptures in the Bible, or other inspirational books. The more we feed our minds, with positive thoughts, the easier it is to control our thinking.

Affirmations have an incredible effect on our minds. When we continue to say positive statements about ourselves, they become internalized and embedded in our subconscious, which causes them to be manifested. Our words materialize into our reality. In order to be victorious, we must make positive affirmations a daily ritual or habit. They create the positive energy we need to charge us up and to increase our self-esteem. They are the nuggets of wisdom that open the doors for good things to come into our lives. They empower us! If we want to change what happens in our lives, we must change what we believe. Daily affirmations give us our own foundation of truth. They influence our belief.

Recognize your goals and turn them into affirmations. Write them down. Tape them up around the house. Make it a daily practice to get up and recite to yourself who you want to become. Speak your affirmations in the present tense, i.e. "I am successful," "I am rich," "I am beautiful." The Bible tells us to speak things that are not as though they were. When we do this, we are essentially ordering in advance what we desire. The universe will give us back our desired results. Speak what you want into existence! Don't wait for good things to come, send for them through your words!

Words are powerful. The power of life and death lies in the tongue. As we become the master of our thoughts, we will also become the master of our words. When we begin to understand how powerful our words are, we will no longer speak words of negativity over our lives. Negative phrases include: "I can't do it," "I'll never get that type of job," and "I will always fail." When we make these statements, we give them power to become our reality.

Think about the late Tupac Shakur and the Notorious "BIG." They were both rappers who spoke their death into existence, by naming their albums and songs titles such as, "Ready to Die." They spoke their raps with such passion and feeling that they dictated to the universe "this is my desired result," and look what happened. They both ended up dead. This is a powerful demonstration of the power of words. Watch what you say and what you think!

Negative thoughts not only affect our future, but they also have a direct effect on our health. The body is the servant of our mind. It obeys the commands our mind gives it. When we are filled with negative thoughts, the body responds by producing disease and decay. Disease and health are rooted in thought. Thoughts of sickness will express themselves through a sick body. Strong, pure, positive thoughts build up the body. Many people have allowed thoughts of envy, jealousy, hate and other ill will to confine them to a self-made prison of bad physical health. As our thoughts change, we will see our health change, too. Positive thoughts create positive energy to maintain good health.

One of our greatest tools is in the power of imagination, which is also known as visualization. As we are able to picture success in our minds, and are able to feel the feelings of our desired results, we summon what we imagine into our lives. Each day you should spend at least 15 minutes picturing yourself living the life you dream of having. Your mind is the boomerang that brings you your desired results. Use your mind. It is your greatest weapon. Conquer it, or it will conquer you!

Let's close this chapter with an affirmation to help channel positive thoughts into our lives: *"Today I understand how important it is to think positively. Whatever I allow myself to think will become my reality. Therefore, I take authority over my mind. I recognize my mind as a gift from God, and I will use it wisely. I will discipline my mind by watching my thoughts. I will consistently feed my mind with positive thoughts. I will read uplifting inspirational books, and I will surround myself with positive people. Whenever I start to feel negative emotions such as anger, depression or sadness, I will use them as a clue that it is time to change channels in my mind. Then, I will purposely release my negative thoughts and inject positive thoughts through affirmations and visualization. I will no longer allow myself to wallow in hopelessness and depression. I will take charge of my day, and I will experience the goodness of it. Therefore, I will diligently look for a positive outcome in every situation. I am grateful. I am blessed. I will thank God everyday for all my wonderful blessings, and He will bless me with more. I am happy because I control my destiny and my joy. I am the master of my thoughts."*

Now let's close this chapter with a short prayer: *"God, I thank You for bringing me into the enlightenment of the power that is within me. I ask that You continue to give me wisdom and knowledge. Direct me and guide me on my journey to liberation. Help me keep my mind cleansed and pure. Help me to control and take authority over the negative thoughts that come my way. Allow me to experience peace, happiness and joy. Amen."*

CHAPTER QUESTIONS

1) Why is it important to maintain positive thoughts?
2) Explain in your own words what the law of attraction is?
3) What are the results of an attitude of gratitude?
4) Why is it dangerous to speak negative words?
5) Name three ways to eliminate negative thinking.

WRITING ASSIGNMENT

Write down your own personalized affirmations of the steps you will use to change your thinking, based on what you learned in Chapter 3. Commit to this affirmation and recite it daily. You will be amazed by the results you achieve.

CHAPTER 4

The Power of Recognizing Your Purpose

Many of us have traveled through life aimlessly. We have searched for fulfillment, sincerely believing that people, places and things would provide the solution. "When I find my husband, life will be great." "When I get this amount of money and move over there, I won't have any more troubles." Believing we had the solution to our problems, we persistently sought our so-called avenues to fulfillment. Many of us obtained them, only to discover they didn't bring us the joy we so desperately anticipated. Disappointed, we went back to the drawing board and began again. "Okay, now let me get this car and I'll be happy." "Once I have this job, I'll be set." Or, "when I gain them as my friends, things will work out." We pursued our new idols. Some of us obtained them, too, only to come to the same discovery—they didn't fulfill us either. Even now, many of us are still misled. We have gone through life without properly assessing our true priorities. Our focus is distorted. We are seeking things as our first priority. External things will never have the power to fulfill us. It's like a dog chasing his tail; he will never catch it.

There is only one way to be truly satisfied in life. Only one thing can fulfill our inner desires and ambition. This powerful instrument is called purpose. Purpose is finding God's intended plan for your life and living it.

Each of us is a unique, wonderful creature, designed with specific gifts and talents. We all were created to do work here on earth that will bring honor to our Higher Power. It is our job to discover what this purpose is and to pursue it passionately. There is no feeling in the world that can compare to living according to your purpose. It's like a race car built to excel at high speeds. You can drive the car around the neighborhood and it will perform its function, but what a waste that is. This car was built to travel at high speeds. The engine was specifically designed to perform when racing. There are parts in this car that will remain dormant until the car is driven at high speeds. It is only when you get on the highway and accelerate that you will see the awesome power of the car. All the instruments used to build the race car will ignite, and the car will perform at a higher rate than any regular car. It is the same with us. When we tap into what we were created to do, we will become successful, performing at the peak of our abilities. When we do what we are created to do best, our light begins to shine and brightens the lives of others. Experiencing this power gives us the esteem, honor and the fulfillment that we have been seeking. The majority of our problems, as we know them today, will disappear when we find purpose. Purpose is power!

When I was first challenged to discover my purpose, I begin to read Rick Warren's *The Purpose Driven Life*. This book led me to the understanding of true purpose. I will share some of these principles in the chapters to come. I suggest after reading this book, you pick up a copy of *The Purpose Driven Life*. It will give you further instruction and guidance in discovering your purpose.

Purpose is not just about your own personal fulfillment or your happiness. It's greater than you and your personal ambitions. Purpose is based on being harmoniously connected with our Higher Power. It is fulfilling His will and His desire for our lives. Purpose is not discovered by focusing on "self." Purpose is discovered by selflessly focusing on God. It is only through our communion with Him that we discover our identity, our meaning, our significance, and our purpose. Any other path will lead to disappointment.

Being successful according to the world's standards does not fulfill your life's purpose. Purpose is not about the car you drive, the home you live in or the husband you have. You could reach all your personal goals in life and be looked at by others as a shining star, yet still miss the mark of purpose. Think about the celebrities you see on television. They look so happy. They have fame and fortune, and they seem to be successful, yet you see many of them abusing drugs and attempting suicide. Why? One of the worst feelings is setting goals based on the belief that external things will fulfill your inner void, only to accomplish them and discover you are still empty inside. It makes life feel useless and purposeless. That's why we see so many suicidal, depressed, unhappy people. They have missed the mark! People, places and things can never completely satisfy us. Our inner void is only filled by realizing God's purpose.

Life becomes manageable when we are able to develop focus. Our focus should be on what matters most in life. When purpose is discovered, we can move with precision and courage, accomplishing what we were destined to do. When we discover purpose, we are no longer chasing meaningless things. We become focused on the agenda our Partner has created us to do. When we accomplish this assignment, we feel fulfilled. We are rewarded with the joy that only our Higher Power can give. When He is pleased with us, He shines His light upon us. We feel the power of His radiance, which keeps us joyful and energized and able to perform vigorously. With this power, we can do what we never dreamed we could accomplish. Purpose is powerful!

It is no accident, coincidence or mistake that you are here this day, reading this book in your situation. God has a plan. He knew where, and in what position, He needed to have you in order to gain your attention. "When the student is ready, the teacher will come," is a truthful proverb. Everything had to happen in the sequence it occurred in. Now you are ready to walk into your purpose!

It is after we do all we can do as humans, and then fail, that we are able to realize we don't have all the answers. Have you ever been on a road trip with a stubborn person who refuses to ask for directions? You repeatedly suggest the person stop at a gas station or ask a pedestrian for directions and they refuse. "No, I know where I'm going. I've been here before. So-and-so came this way and I watched Him. He found it, I can find it, too." So they continue to go around and around in circles. After you see the same store four or five times, you finally become frustrated and convince the person to stop for assistance. Then, you both discover the place you were looking for was right around the corner. In fact, you had passed the block several times and didn't even know it. This analogy represents the lifestyles of many of us. We have been so stubborn that we failed to simply seek help. This mistake has landed us in our current situation.

When we surrender and accept the fact that we need help to successfully complete our mission, then we can call on our Higher Power. He will reveal to us our purpose through His divine revelations. Without knowing this purpose, life is trivial, petty, and pointless. We must make a choice: Either we continue to wander aimlessly, or we stop and ask for help.

According to Rick Warren, purpose has five great benefits:

1) **Knowing your purpose gives meaning to your life.** We were created to perform a certain task on Earth. Performing this task brings meaning to our lives.

When life has meaning you can bear almost anything. Without purpose, life is meaningless. In this state, obstacles will lead us into a frenzy of self-destruction. Suicidal thoughts come when we feel life is meaningless or has no purpose. Discovering purpose can spark life back into what seemed to be a hopeless existence. One of the greatest misfortunes in life is not death, but life without purpose. Hope is essential to life. We need hope to shield us from the fiery darts of life. Purpose brings hope. Hope offers joy even in the midst of our storms. When we discover our purpose, we open the prison doors of life that caged us. Purpose will make prison bearable. When you discover there's purpose in your pain, you can bear it. You can smile when others around you cry. You can remain happy knowing your obstacle was the necessary bridge to take you where you needed to go so you could soar in life.

2) **Knowing your purpose simplifies your life.** When we discover our purpose it shifts our priorities. It helps us to clearly define the boundaries of what we will or will not allow. When we know our purpose and are focused on accomplishing it, we will protect it. We won't allow distractions to intrude and take us away from what we must accomplish. It gives us the strength we need to avoid the wrong choices that jeopardize the goal of fulfilling our purpose. Without a clear purpose, we have no foundation on which to base our decisions, to allocate our time and to utilize our resources. We tend to make bad choices when we are clueless about our mission. In a clueless state, we are controlled by our emotions and circumstances rather than our knowledge. People who do not know

their focus try to do too much. This causes stress, fatigue and conflict. Therefore, by being driven by purpose leads to a simpler, more enjoyable life.

3) **Knowing your purpose focuses your life.** When you discover your purpose you are able to concentrate your effort and energy on what you do best. Without clear purpose we tend to keep changing directions, jobs, relationships, etc – hoping each will settle our confusion and fill our emptiness. With purpose, we are able to aim and hit our target instead of shooting amiss. There is nothing as powerful as a focused life! The men and women who have achieved the greatest accomplishments in history were the ones who were most focused. They accurately targeted, aimed and hit. They are no different than you and I. The difference is they were focused, they knew their purpose, and they accomplished it!

4) **Knowing your purpose motivates you in your life.** The most powerful energy from within is passion. Passion can create supernatural change. It is the energy that motivates us to accomplish our mission with excellence. Passion makes work fun and effortless. It makes a job a desire rather than a duty. When we know our purpose we discover our passion. Passion is the energy necessary to sustain us even in the midst of challenges. Passion will overcome every obstacle that stands in its way. People who lack motivation have not yet tapped into their inner passion. When you are driven by passion, you will discover success.

5) **Knowing your purpose prepares you for eternity.** Our life here on Earth is a temporary assignment. Life is a test; our scores, or achievements

on Earth, determine our placement in eternity. Life is temporary. Eternity is forever. When we are able to retain and understand that revelation, we discover that the things we thought were so important are not as significant as we assumed. All achievement on Earth will eventually pass. Our focus should be on obtaining a good relationship with our Higher Power and on building an eternal legacy. All that we do on Earth should be to please God, not people. When we start prioritizing that which is ultimately most important, we will obtain victory in our everyday lives.

Now that we understand the importance of purpose and its benefits, let's discover the attributes of purpose.

We were all put on Earth to make a contribution. We weren't created to consume or to take up space. We were created to serve God. We serve God by serving His people. What task do you perform best that you like to do that also helps mankind? Think about the joy you receive deep down inside when you are able to do something that benefits others, and they express their gratitude to you. Life is not all about you. It's about helping other people. When we help others, we send a great force of energy to the universe that will in turn send great help back to us. Success in life comes from finding the gift, talent, or skill set you are best at that gives back to society. When you operate in this gift, it will bring you deep joy and satisfaction from within.

Listen to your heart. Your heart will lead you to discover your purpose. God equips us with the gift of desire. He places in our hearts the desire to perform certain tasks. This desire never moves. We may temporarily suppress it, but it always remains. At times, the feeling is very intense. What has been in your heart to do for a very long time? Even if you don't believe you can achieve it, recall this desire. God has a plan for you. Whatever you desire to do that is in His will, He will help you accomplish it by sending you the necessary resources to bring it to life. Never neglect your dreams and your desires. Pray about them and visualize them, then God will bring them to past!

What do you do that brings you great enthusiasm and enjoyment? What do others compliment you on and say you do best? What asset do you possess that you feel is most helpful to others? These are the questions you must ponder to discover your purpose.

Many of us have hidden talents and abilities that we are unaware of. We must start doing what is in our hearts that we never did before. Today you have permission to dream. You will never discover your purpose without utilizing your ability to dream. Close your eyes and picture yourself being the person you want to be. Now, take your tragedy and turn it into triumph!

In the first chapter, we discussed the power of learning from our past. It is our past hardships that will lead us to discover our purpose. It was God's plan for many of us to suffer certain hardships, so we will develop the compassion and ability to help someone else overcome the same dilemmas. God uses prisons to heal and restore His chosen people so they can empower others. Have you ever thought about using your story to help someone else avoid the road that you took? Are you good at talking to others and persuading them to see things from your point of view? If so, there is a good chance that your life is purposed to help others in the field of Human Services. You could be a counselor, a director or even a creator of a program that helps people overcome life's obstacles.

Whatever you choose to do to fulfill your purpose, do it with passion. Perform with excellence! You will feel happy from within, and your work will support and uplift others. Why waste time and energy? Get focused, and discover why you were created to live on this Earth at this time. When you discover purpose, your life will never be the same.

Now that you understand the importance of discovering your purpose, are you ready for change? If so, let's take this time to ask God to reveal His perfect plan to you: *"God, I thank You for placing me where I am at this time, for me to understand my need to know my purpose. I've tried in many ways to find fulfillment, only to fail. I understand today that true fulfillment comes when I discover Your intended plan for my life, so today I ask You to please reveal my gifts, my talents, my abilities and my purpose. Make it clear and plain for me to see, and I will follow Your directions. I now open my heart to hear Your answer. Amen."*

Congratulations, you have opened the door for God's plan to be revealed to you. What you experience from Him in revelation will amaze you! Now you will start to understand so much that seemed foreign to you before. Your purpose will also reveal why you had to go through all that you have endured to get to this point. This understanding will ease your pain and bring you joy.

Purpose cannot be discovered overnight. It is a fine-tuning process that takes time and requires some work on our part. Let's close this chapter with an affirmation so we can stay focused on discovering our purpose: *"Today I realize the power of recognizing my purpose. I have been put on this Earth to fulfill a specific duty that will bring glory to God. I eagerly wish to know this purpose, so I will daily seek to discover it. I will assess all my strengths and my talents. I will discover what I'm good at and what I like to do. I will learn from others the things I do that bring them joy. I am determined. I will not stop searching until I discover my purpose."*

Say this affirmation daily and practice what you preach. If you are persistent, you will discover purpose. Purpose will bring you everything you have been looking for and more! Never forget the key to a successful life is living with purpose. May you find what you are in search of and soar like an eagle all the days of your life!

CHAPTER QUESTIONS

1) Why is discovering your purpose important?
2) What is life like without purpose?
3) Describe in your own words Rick Warren's five benefits of purpose.
4) How do you discover your purpose?
5) Why is pursuit of the world's idea of success not necessarily fulfilling purpose?

WRITING ASSIGNMENT

a) Write down a list of all your gifts, talents and abilities.
b) Describe your personality and the strengths in your character.
c) List three things you have done for others that were meaningful and positively affected their lives.
d) Based on your answers to the previous questions, take your best guess and write down what you believe you were born to do. This statement should reflect what you believe your purpose is here on Earth.

CHAPTER 5

The Power of Developing Good Habits

I n the pursuit to discovering our purpose, we must prepare ourselves to reach the mark. This requires work, dedication and persistence. It also requires us to change our lifestyle. To be successful, we must do what successful people do. We can want a better life, but until we add action to our desire we will remain stagnant in the same state.

The position you are in today did not develop overnight. It is the result of patterns and practices you acquired throughout your life. These patterns molded your existence as you know it today. These patterns have been embedded in your mind, so they are now natural and normal to you. You may not even be aware of many of them; it is hard to fix what you cannot see.

In this chapter, we will identify bad habits and explore good habits and their benefits. This chapter will give you the information you need to examine negative thought patterns and character flaws that have stagnated your growth. Change only occurs when you change your thinking. Now we will program our minds for success. We will see the habits successful people practice, and we will apply them to our lives. We will also identify our bad habits and learn how to quickly discard them, so they no longer hinder us from reaching our dreams.

Life does not just happen. The choices we make and our responses to our dilemmas shape and form our existence.

43

Destiny is not a matter of chance; it is based on our choices. It is the actions we choose to make today that determine our future outcome. The key to success is to change our actions, which form our habits. A habit is the actions you become accustomed to taking, which you give little thought. Habits are the behavior patterns that you repeat so often that they become automatic. As human beings we all are creatures of habit. Up to 90% of our behavior is based on habits. Many of our day-to-day activities are simply a routine that we have created. Habits do not have to be permanent. We can deprogram and reprogram ourselves at any time simply by changing our actions.

It is a common belief that successful people achieve their goals because of luck. This theory is simply incorrect. Successful people don't just shoot to the top. It is their actions, focus, discipline and perseverance that get them there, and keep them there. There are lucky people in the world who do shoot to the top, but usually just as quickly they will fall. Their failure results from not having the skill set necessary to maintain long-term success. Without a proper foundation and the ability to manage wealth, wealth is quickly lost. Let's think about people who win the lottery, or attain some other quick form of fame, and who acquire a large amount of money at one time. If you examine the lives of these people a year or two later, many are left back at their starting point, with nothing. Why? Their foundation was not solid. They didn't have the discipline or the knowledge needed to maintain their fortune. We will not be like them! Let's utilize our time of incarceration wisely and learn the key strategies to obtaining success. This time, let's build our house with bricks. Then, when hardships arise or if the big bad wolf comes to blow our house down, we will be safe. We will survive!

There are no shortcuts to success. Shortcuts will always lead us back to the same point we were at before we achieved our accomplishments—the beginning. Therefore, we must roll up our sleeves and do things the correct way, so we don't have to repeat the same course.

Growing up, I remember the local drug dealers on the corner laughing about the young boy who decided to work at McDonald's as a "fry guy," as they called him. This boy worked hard, paid his way through college and became the manager of McDonald's. Eight years later, he purchased the same McDonald's from the previous owner. The boys who laughed at him had very different destinies. Some are in prison, and a few of them are dead. The rest are struggling with low paying jobs. In the end, the "fry guy" had the last laugh. He became successful because he was willing to work hard at it. He had the wisdom to make sacrifices so he could be successful in the future. The local drug dealers were unsuccessful because they sought instant gratification. They wanted a quick, "microwave" fix. Remember, all shortcuts are short-lived. Think of them as a beautiful house built on a weak foundation. The house may look stunning, and you might even get to live in it. But, as soon as you become comfortable living in that house, it will surely collapse. God forbid you are inside when it crumbles, as you are sure to be destroyed with it! It is the same with all shortcuts that bring instant gratification. I bet the guy who laughed at the "fry guy," who is now sitting in prison, would give anything to trade places with the "fry guy." Seeing the end result, the imprisoned man is able to realize how destructive his bad choices were. Let's not have any further regrets. Let's get things right and succeed in life.

We can turn negative consequences into positive rewards simply by changing our habits. It takes approximately 21 days or 3-4 weeks to establish new habits. We can begin today. In a short time, the results you see will amaze you! Certain habits are easy to change, others are deeply embedded. Some bad habits will take time and concentrated effort to derail. We also must be on guard that, when we do successfully change our habits, we don't slip back into the same old patterns when stress arises or unexpected circumstances come; it is easy to stray from your plans. Be alert and vigilant! Don't let anyone or anything stop you from staying focused on achieving your dreams.

Before we can change our habits, we must first identify them. In the book, *The Power of Focus,* authors Jack Canfield, Mark Victor Hansen, and Les Hewitt list the 24 principal bad habits of unsuccessful people. These habits are:

1) Not returning phone calls on time.
2) Being late for meetings and appointments.
3) Poor communication with others.
4) A lack of clarity about expected outcomes, monthly targets, goals, etc.
5) Not allowing enough travel time for outside appointments.
6) Not attending to work quickly and efficiently.
7) Allowing bills to go unpaid.
8) Talking instead of listening.
9) Forgetting someone's name sixty seconds (or less) after being introduced.
10) Hitting the snooze alarm several times in the morning before getting out of bed (oversleeping).
11) Working long days with no exercise or regular breaks.
12) Not spending enough time with your children.
13) Having a fast food meal program Monday through Friday.
14) Eating at irregular times of the day.
15) Leaving home in the morning without hugging your wife, husband, children and/or dog.

16) Taking work home with you.
17) Socializing too much on the telephone.
18) Making reservations or plans at the last minute.
19) Not following through on time as promised with other people's requests.
20) Not taking enough time off for fun and family.
21) Having your cell phone on at all times.
22) Answering the telephone during family meal times.
23) Controlling every decision, especially the small stuff you need to let go!
24) Procrastination on everything from filing taxes to cleaning out your garage.

I also created a list of common bad habits among incarcerated women. These 20 bad habits, which most of us are guilty of, are listed below:

1) Hanging out with the wrong people.
2) Not counting the cost of your decisions before making them.
3) Spending too much time watching television and doing other activities that add no value to your life.
4) Smoking, drinking and doing drugs to relieve the pressures and pains of your life.
5) Starting and not finishing projects and activities.
6) Lying instead of accepting responsibility.
7) Not being a woman of your word!
8) Depending on people to do what you can do for yourself.
9) Procrastination. Always looking for the easy way out.
10) Not taking full responsibility for your choices.

11) Not spending enough time with God, in prayer, meditation and reading the Word.
12) Complaining about what you don't have and not being grateful for what you do have.
13) Not planning and organizing your goals in a manageable written system.
14) Allowing your mind to focus on negative thoughts.
15) Not doing the work to find out what you need to know to succeed in life.
16) Letting others control you by basing your life on their opinions and perspectives.
17) Relying on people, places and things for happiness, and basing your happiness on the energy and happiness of others.
18) Not believing in yourself.
19) Not controlling your emotions.
20) Not protecting and caring for your own well-being.

Now that you have a list of the common bad habits of unproductive people in society and amongst imprisoned women, analyze both of these lists and determine which bad habits you have adopted in life. It is important that you are honest with yourself. That is the only way you can accurately pinpoint your weaknesses and open the door to change. Also, take time out to think of any additional bad habits you may have established in your life. Record them in your Workbook/Journal so you can be aware of what other characteristics you need to work on. Until you clearly understand what habits are holding you back, you cannot take the necessary actions to move ahead in life.

Another way of identifying your bad habits is to ask others

whom you trust, that will be honest with you, to give you feedback on the bad habits you may have demonstrated in the past. Remember, you are building a new house. We are starting from the ground up. It is necessary that we remove all the damaged rubbish, the faulty beams and the broken pipes, so we can replace them. One faulty pipe could destroy the entire structure; so we must be careful, take our time and identify our damaged areas. Then, replace them with new products that will work!

Once you have identified your bad or unproductive habits, it's time that you identify solutions that will allow you to change them. Once you find the solutions, create a plan of action to bring about these changes. Usually the solution to your bad habit is to do the exact opposite, i.e. if you have been going to work late, the plan of action is to go to bed early, have your clothes out the night before and get up 30 minutes earlier than you normally do. This will enable you to leave earlier and get to work on time. Nothing will change until you take action!

Now I will take the two lists of bad habits that we reviewed earlier in this chapter and create a list of good habits we can adapt to negate the bad habits previously listed:

THE POWER OF FOCUS; BAD HABITS LIST REVERSED TO GOOD HABITS

1) Returning phone calls promptly
2) Being early or on time for meetings.
3) Communicating well with others.
4) Being clear about the expectancy of outcomes, monthly targets, goals, etc.
5) Allowing more than enough travel time to get where you have to go.
6) Paying the bills before they are due, or at least on time.

7) Listening carefully to others before talking.
8) Doing your work quickly and efficiently and completing assignments on time.
9) Remembering people's names when they are introduced.
10) Getting up early or on time.
11) Exercising and taking regular breaks throughout the day.
12) Spending adequate time with your children.
13) Eating healthy, home-cooked meals.
14) Eating at regular times of the day.
15) Hugging your children and loved ones when leaving the house in the morning.
16) Not taking work home with you.
17) Monitoring the time you spend talking on the phone.
18) Making plans and reservations ahead of time.
19) Following through on time when meeting the requests of others.
20) Taking time out for fun and family.
21) Turning off your cell phones at appropriate times.
22) Not answering the phone during family meals.
23) Letting others make some decisions so you don't feel overwhelmed by the small stuff.
24) Taking care of tasks quickly and not letting them pile up.

Here's the list of good habits that negate the common bad habits of incarcerated women:

GOOD HABITS FOR INCARCERATED WOMEN

1) Associating with positive people who encourage and uplift you.
2) Counting and assessing in advance the consequences of your actions.
3) Scheduling a moderate amount of time for television programs and allowing yourself time to read, study and to do other productive things.
4) Managing your emotions and fully dealing with problems and feelings so you do not have to resort to smoking, drinking or doing drugs to relieve pressure and stress.
5) Completing the tasks you start.
6) Making honesty your only policy and taking responsibility for your actions without making up excuses.
7) Becoming a woman of your word. Do what you say you will do at the time you promised to do it.
8) Not depending on people to do the things you can do for yourself.
9) Working hard and persevering as you move towards your goals.
10) Taking full responsibility for all your choices, even if it means suffering the consequences.
11) Spending time with God daily in prayer, meditation and by reading the Word.
12) Being grateful and giving thanks for the things you do have and waiting patiently for more good to come.

13) Planning and organizing your life by setting goals and reaching them.

14) Keeping your mind steadfast on positive thoughts.

15) Researching and studying ways to obtain your goals.

16) Not letting the opinions of others alter your destiny; becoming a pleaser of God rather than pleaser of people.

17) Coming into self-awareness and studying and caring for self, so you can rely on yourself to create happiness.

18) Believing in yourself.

19) Protecting yourself and creating boundaries so others cannot impose their wills upon you.

Now that we have assessed the good habits we need to adopt, there is only one thing left for us to do-act upon them. In your *Voices of Consequences* Workbook/Journal, identify your bad habits, write out the good habits that will negate the bad ones, and create a 3-step action plan that you will use to change your bad habits into your new, good habits. Create an action plan for each bad habit you possess. As you change these habits and put your action plan to work, you are going to develop into a new, improved self! These habits will lead you to the doorway of success.

Are you ready to change your life by changing your habits? If so, let's get some help and assistance along the way. Let's pray: *"God, I thank You for bringing me into awareness of my destructive habits. I also thank You for providing me with knowledge of the solution I can use to change them. Now I ask You to give me the strength, wisdom and support that I need to change. Awaken me to know when I'm doing the wrong things. Help me to stay on the right track to my divine destiny. Send people into my life who will help me in my mission of change and who will support my goals. Help me break every negative habit that has kept me bound. I now claim my success. I thank You for my new life. Amen."*

Creating new successful habits will take persistence and dedication, but now we have help from our Higher Power to accomplish this goal. We are destined to succeed. Let's close this chapter with an affirmation to keep focused on the work we must do to improve our habits: *"Today I am a new creature that possesses good habits. Each day I will analyze and assess the habits that are not good for the advancement of my life. When I recognize these habits, I will immediately write them down and determine the solution. I will create a plan to change them, and I will act on this plan immediately. I will no longer be controlled by adverse decisions and choices. I will plan ahead and count the cost of my actions. I will make good choices. I will learn from my mistakes and immediately correct them. I will succeed. I am a woman whose life is organized and successful because of my good habits."*

CHAPTER QUESTIONS

1) What is a habit?
2) How long does it take to develop a habit?
3) What are the effects of bad habits?
4) Why are successful people able to maintain their success?
5) How do you change a bad habit into a good one?

WRITING ASSIGNMENT

After you make a list of all your bad habits and of the good habits you will replace them with, make your own personal affirmation. State your new positive goals and what you will do daily to achieve them.

CHAPTER 6

The Power of Organized Planning

As we have journeyed down the road of empowerment, we have become conscious of the many essential ingredients we need to achieve our dreams. We've learned how to gain an advantage by taking our Higher Power on as our Partner. We've learned the techniques and strategies to keep our minds refreshed with positive thinking. We've learned how to tap into discovering purpose, and we've learned principles to detect our bad habits, and to uproot them and establish good habits. We are halfway through our journey. Now it's time to learn how to take all of our findings and turn them into an organized plan.

We have all had ideas and dreams in our past that we've wished to accomplish. Many of us have pursued these dreams and, after some effort, have failed. Not understanding the techniques of successful people, others opted to quit. But it wasn't our plan or our idea that was the problem; instead, we lacked an accurate, organized plan. Nothing can be accomplished without a plan. A plan is a detailed, written map that provides direction on how we will get to where we need to go. It includes the "Five Ws:" who, what, where, when and why. It is the instrument we use to become aware of what we will have to do in order to accomplish our dreams. When we have a plan and follow it, the process keeps us grounded and prevents distractions from taking us off course.

It is a common belief that we can just plan in our minds, and we don't need to put our plans on paper. This is simply foolish. A real plan needs to include strategy. You cannot create strategies without visually counting the cost. When you put your plan on paper, it requires you to think and to expand on your idea. A good plan details cost and reveals hidden factors that you may not have anticipated. It also provides alternatives: If plan A does not work, I can still accomplish plan B. Every successful person is a strategist. They prepare themselves for unforeseen difficulties, so they will be able to weather the storms of life. We must do the same by creating an organized plan that includes the step-by-step details of what we must do to get ahead in life.

In order to achieve our dreams, we must spend time regularly thinking and planning how we can have a better future. Taking time to think (which is a form of meditation) is essential to our success. Many of us have learned to become excellent at worrying. We spend endless hours thinking about how something bad may happen. We need to negate that bad habit by spending quality time thinking and planning our futures. We start this process in meditation. Close your eyes and see yourself where you are now. Then, picture yourself where you want to be. Like a caterpillar changing into a butterfly, see yourself transforming into the woman you dream to be. Stay in the moment and become this woman. Live this experience in detail in your imagination. Stand as she stands. Look as she looks. Feel as she feels. Go to the places she goes. Live as she lives. As you spend time in your mind being the new you, you are opening up your thoughts and consciousness to lead you onto that path. Visualization is such an important tool. It awakens our minds to be able to create an organized plan complete with details, because through visualization we focus and clearly see what we would like to achieve.

After you have a crystal-clear picture in your mind of what you want, the next step is to start creating goals. A goal is what you expect to achieve at a particular time. A goal can be as simple as setting aside 15 minutes a day to read, or as big as earning your Master's degree. Your goals are your dreams. They can be big or small. Setting goals is a process that helps to measure your growth and progress. When followed, goals motivate us to accomplish our expectations. Goals are tools for success. We need them to outline in our minds what we must do to get to where we want to go. Goals keep us on track, and provide the road map to get us to our desired destination.

Now it's time to get out your paper and your pen. Let's start creating some goals that we want to accomplish to achieve our dreams. First, let me share with you the top 10 goals checklist excerpted from the book, *The Power of Focus*, by Jack Canfield, Mark Victor Hansen, and Les Hewitt. You can use this list to better define your goals.

THE TOP-10 GOALS CHECKLIST

1) **Your most important goals must be yours.** You cannot let others define what your goals in life will be. They must be derived from your own will and your own thoughts. When we set goals that other people want for us, we tend not to be motivated to achieve them. It takes desire and drive to achieve goals. If the goal is not your own, you may get halfway through and quit because you have no passion to move forward. Think about how many people in this world are miserable because they are working in occupations they never wanted to pursue. Have you ever been to a place, maybe a store or even the hospital, and when you approached a clerk or staff member to seek help,

that person was rude and inconsiderate? Maybe the person was also impatient, constantly watching the clock, waiting to get off work. From that person's actions, you could clearly tell he or she was not happy working at that job. This is a miserable way to live. It is another form of imprisonment. Don't allow this to happen to you. Set goals of your own that you are passionate about. Do the things that bring you joy regardless of what others may say.

2) **Your goals must be meaningful.** Your goals need substance. They must produce a good result. Commitment is a crucial ingredient if you want to achieve your dreams. You cannot be committed to something you don't fully believe in. When listing your goals, ask yourself: "What's really important to me? What's my purpose in doing this? What am I prepared to give up to make this happen?" When you consider these questions, you will weed out the goals that you are not really committed to. Also, analyze the rewards and benefits of your goals. These rewards can motivate you to stay committed and focused on accomplishing your goals. Remember, accomplishing your dreams will take discipline. Discipline requires commitment. When we commit ourselves to an action plan we must clearly identify the rewards that come from our discipline, as well as the regrets that will come if we quit. This analysis will keep us focused on our prize.

3) **Your goals must be specific and measurable.** Goals must be detailed and not general. They must not leave any space for compromise. One of the main reasons why people don't achieve what they are capable of doing is because they don't accurately define what

they want. When you go to a restaurant you don't tell the waitress to bring you a sandwich, a slice of cake and a soda. You are specific. You may order a chicken sandwich, a piece of chocolate cake and a Pepsi. How would you feel if you worked hard and paid for a meal but got food you didn't like? It's the same with goals. We must be specific to gain our desired results. Get to the point. Use the details you see in your visualization. By being specific you will dramatically increase the chances of achieving your desired results. Set deadlines. State specifically what resources you will need, the help you will require, and your expectations.

When you have big goals, such as becoming a business owner, take your large goal and break it down into smaller goals. For example, my goal is to become a business owner. I will accomplish this by making contact with other business owners, reading books about business and taking some college courses. You can also turn this one broad goal into four goals that detail your action plan by getting even more specific, i.e. I will own my own computer business in five years. I will read approximately 20 books on computer technology and entrepreneurship. I will meet at least three other people who own computer companies. I will obtain my associate's degree in computer science. The more specific you are, the better you can plan, and the greater your success rate will be.

4) **Your goals must be flexible.** You want to include some alternatives just in case Plan A doesn't work. You don't want a plan that is so rigid you feel suffocated by it. Your goals should be realistic and enjoyable. A flexible plan gives you freedom to divert your plans if

an opportunity arises for you to go in another direction. That is not to say that you need to keep changing directions, but their maybe exceptions. You should analyze each possible detour as it comes. If it is a solid opportunity and you thoroughly check it out, go for it!

5) **Your goals must be challenging and exciting.** Your goals need to stimulate you and be enjoyable at the same time. When your goals have an edge, they keep you from getting bored and from abandoning your plan. Force yourself out of your comfort zone. Dare to do the things you've dreamed of doing but never thought you could accomplish! Push yourself to go the extra mile, and make your plans challenging and fun.

6) **Your goals must be in alignment with your values.** Each of us has core beliefs and values. They are the morals that we live by and are passionate about. When our goals are aligned with our core values, we create harmony and synergy. When our goals uphold the values we believe in, we will become more passionate about achieving them. When you set goals that contradict your intuition or your gut feelings, you will be apprehensive about acting on them, causing you to fail even before you begin. When you harness your core values to positive, exciting, purposeful goals, you will find decision-making easy. You don't have to suffer an internal conflict. When you set integral goals from within, you know that what you are doing is right. It stands for what you believe in, so you gladly perform with excellence.

7) **Your goals must be well balanced.** In order to be happy and successful, we must create balance in our lives. There must be time for fun, family and friends.

Goals will overburden you and drain you of energy if they do not include these additions. When setting your goals, make sure you include time to relax and time to enjoy life, as well as time to spend with those whom you love.

8) **Your goals must be realistic.** Do not create goals you know are impossible to achieve at this point. It will only discourage you. Many people are unrealistic about the time it will take to accomplish their goals. Give yourself enough time to achieve the accomplishments you want. There is no such thing as an unrealistic goal. There are only unrealistic time-frames to accomplish certain goals. Allow yourself a reasonable amount of time to develop into the person you dream to become.

9) **Your goals must include contribution.** As we discussed in Chapter 4, our purpose on this Earth is centered on providing service to others. Our goals must reflect that belief. Success is not about money and material things, it is about serving God. When we provide the service we are created to give, then we reach fulfillment. Achieving fulfillment is true success. Contribution can be given in several forms. We can give our time, our experience or expertise, and we can also give our money. Giving back should always be a part of our goals. When we give, we should not expect an immediate payback or return. As we plant the seed of giving, we are sure to reap a harvest. Our harvest will come back in many unimaginable ways. If we don't give, we have not planted. It is impossible to receive without giving first. Make giving a top priority and blessings will surely come!

10) **Your goals need to be supported.** In order for us to stay encouraged, we must have people around us who support us and encourage us to move forward. We may encounter times when we feel discouraged due to life's various obstacles. It is during these times that we need a push to make it over the hump. Our supporters are our cheerleaders. They help give us the strength we need to push forward. Additionally, we need people to help us achieve our goals. We will need others at times to offer their advice or expertise. Surround yourself with supportive people, and it will be much easier to get where you want to go.

Now that you know what your goals should consist of, it's time to get out your paper and pen. Open your Workbook/Journal and begin to write out 101 goals you wish to accomplish over the next 10 years. Ask yourself the following questions during the process:

1) What do I want to accomplish?
2) What things do I desire to obtain?
3) Where do I want to live?
4) What contribution to society do I want to make?
5) What kind of person do I want to become?
6) What do I want to learn?
7) Who do I want to spend my time with?
8) How much time do I want to spend having fun?
9) How much do I want to earn, save and invest?
10) What will I do to create optimum health?
11) What places would I like to travel to?
12) What things do I want to do for fun?

Take time as you go through this process. Utilize your visualization techniques. Think about what makes you feel good.

You will be amazed by how this process will help you organize your thoughts and gain a clear focus. Get ready to make a major transformation in your thinking! Stop and record your goals in your Workbook/Journal.

Now that you have on paper a clear plan of what you want to accomplish, you will find it easier to achieve your dreams. There is still work to do. But at least you know what goals you desire to achieve. Knowing is half the battle. Now that we know what we want to achieve, let's get some assistance from our Partner to accomplish our goals. Let's pray: *"God, we thank You for helping us to see what we desire to achieve in life. We know based on our own strength, we can do nothing. Therefore, we ask for Your assistance in achieving our goals. Help us to stay focused. Give us the strength we need to accomplish them. Give us the wisdom and knowledge we need to move ahead vigorously. Send us the help and the support we will need to arrive at our divine destiny. Amen."*

Let's close this chapter with an affirmation that will help us stay focused on achieving our goals: *"Today marks a new day for me. Today I know my purpose and what I want to achieve in life. Each day I will work diligently to achieve my goals. I will not let people, places or things distract me from accomplishing my mission. I am determined to succeed! My joy, happiness and fulfillment lie in operating in my divine purpose. Therefore, I will live a purpose-driven life. I see myself as successful. My plans let me know that today I will succeed."*

CHAPTER QUESTIONS

1) What are goals?
2) Why is it important that we write down our plans?
3) Why must our goals be our own?

4) Why must our goals be challenging and exciting?

5) Why must we create a balance in our goals?

WRITING ASSIGNMENT

Now that you have put on paper a clear plan of what you want to accomplish, it's time to organize a more concise breakdown of that plan. From the 101 goals you have listed in your journal and your WRITING ASSIGNMENT #4 (which is a written statement of your purpose), create a concise, clear personal statement. This statement should include who you are, your purpose in life and your major goals that must be achieved to accomplish your mission. Write this statement as an affirmation. Read it daily before you start the day and before you retire to bed at night. If you are faithful in completing this task daily, your dreams will surely come to pass!

CHAPTER 7

The Power of Desire and Faith

We have come a long way in our journey to empowerment. We have an understanding of our purpose and the goals we want to achieve in life. Our minds are focused. We are positioned for success, but in order to achieve our dreams, we must develop two more powerful ingredients of success: desire and faith.

Desire is the passion, the wish or longing for a certain object or accomplishment. It is our inner desires that produce the necessary energy within us to keep us motivated. Faith is the belief in the truth of our mission for success. It is the driving force created within that taps into the universe and brings back our desired results. Without these two ingredients, faith and desire, it is impossible to achieve our dreams. In this Chapter, we will examine the importance of desire and faith and explore techniques to ignite and strengthen these attributes in our lives.

If you don't deeply desire to accomplish your goals, they will not happen. If you don't have faith or deeply believe in yourself and your dream, it will not come to pass. Desire and faith are the two necessary prerequisites to any achievement. They are both vital to successful living. It is imperative that we identify the characteristics of these attributes, as well as understand how to develop techniques that will stimulate a constant flow of desire and faith within us.

Every successful idea or plan begins with a desire. Desire starts as a longing within our hearts to accomplish or obtain something. This feeling may be subtle at first, but it can gradually grow into a deep-rooted passion that tugs on our hearts. Consider advertisements on television for items or products. The first time you see a particular commercial, you say to yourself: "that's interesting." You may even think about it again but toss the idea aside. Later, you go to work and see someone with the item and you think to yourself: "I really like that," but again you dismiss the thought. On your way home, as you turn on the radio, you hear the commercial repeated. Now your desire has increased, but you're still reluctant to act on it. Two days later, your mom comes over with the item, having bought it for herself, and you see your little sister also made the same purchase. This causes your desire to increase. Finally, you decide enough is enough, and your desire draws you to purchase the item.

This example illustrates the function of desire. Desire starts as a seed, but it must be stirred up to create passion. When passion is ignited, desire turns into action. Most people do not succeed in life because of a lack of desire or lack of ambition. If you truly don't want or desire a thing, you will procrastinate acting upon it.

As we discussed in the last chapter, it is important that your goals are your own and not someone else's. If your goals are not created by you, you will lack the necessary desire and drive to obtain them. We are at a crucial point in this journey to empowerment. You must make a decision. Do you truly desire change? Think about it! Until you are committed to the desire to change, your efforts will be worthless. Mommy and Daddy may desire you to change and do everything in their power to make it happen. They can change their occupations to spend more time with you. They can move to another city, and change your school and your church. This is all useless if you don't have the desire to change within. "You can lead a horse to water, but you can't make him drink," is a truthful proverb. Change only occurs when desire is present. Therefore, the question remains: Do you really desire to change your old ways and accomplish your dreams? If you do, continue on this journey of empowerment. That desire is all you need to propel forward to success.

Desire is increased by constant thought. You have to want your dreams so desperately that you are constantly thinking about them. You learned how to meditate and visualize yourself in detail as the woman you dream of becoming. This is a great technique you can utilize throughout the day to get powerful results. We learned how to write affirmations and say them out loud daily. This will also motivate us and program our subconscious minds to act, bringing our goals to pass. Additionally, we wrote out our own personal statement that included our purpose and our goals. This is probably the most powerful written statement we can use to program our minds and our hearts for success. All of the above techniques incite our desires. These are the weapons we use to fight against discouragement, depression and procrastination. When you feel as though you are dragging and are unsure of your future, pull out these weapons and watch your energy reignite!

Now I want to share with you one more technique that will help increase your desire to achieve. Let's create a vision board. Find a piece of cardboard or construction paper; get a pair of scissors and tape or glue. Go through some magazines or newspapers, and cut out all the things you wish to obtain. Cut out the car you want to drive, the house you want to live in, the type of husband you desire and any other images that represent the lifestyle you wish to live. Creatively paste these items on your board. Also, take an old picture of yourself (preferably of you smiling) and place it on this board along with any pictures you may have of family and friends. Create word signs by cutting out words that describe your visualization, i.e. success, happiness, fortune or fame and place them on your collage. Finally, create a bank check written out to yourself in the amount that you desire. You can use the sample check located in the back of your Workbook/Journal. Write out the bank check for the amount of money you dream to have over the next 10 years. Cut this check out and place it in the middle of your board. When you complete this last step, you will have created your own vision board. This is a powerful tool to increase your desire to achieve and keep you focused on your mission.

Faith is the ingredient that turns your inner desires into reality. When faith is mixed with desire, it instantly creates a powerful vibration to the subconscious mind that translates as a prayer to our "Higher Power." It is our faith through prayer that produces results. When you believe you will have something, it will come to you. When you believe you can achieve something, you will succeed and obtain your goal. It's when you don't believe that you destroy your possibilities of obtaining all that you want. In order for us to become successful, we must believe we can be successful. Do you believe in yourself and your dreams?

There will be hard times in life. You will experience difficult days, yet it is during these times that we learn to use our faith to help us overcome. When our faith becomes solid, we are unmovable! With strong faith during times of adversity, we can stare obstacles in the face and say, "It's okay, tomorrow will be better." When people come and say negative words to destroy our dreams, we can laugh and say, "With my Partner I can do all things." Nothing within discourages us or takes us off track, because of our strong faith embedded within. We know that, regardless of our circumstances, we will succeed.

It's important that each of us work on increasing our faith.

Faith comes by hearing positive spoken words. We can increase our faith by studying God's Word, flooding our minds with inspirational and uplifting thoughts, surrounding ourselves with positive people and reading books and testimonies about people who have overcome adversity. As we hear about others who have overcome obstacles, it gives us the faith to believe we can do the same. The worst thing you can do for yourself, especially when you are depressed, is to keep company with negative people. They will instantly contaminate you with their negative thoughts and zap the last bit of positive energy you have left. That is why successful people do not associate with negative people. They don't want the germ of negativity to contaminate their energy. Follow the lead of successful people and stay far away from those who are negative, and those who do not support or believe in your dreams.

The opposite of faith is fear. When we do not have faith, we live in fear. The acronym for fear is: **f**alse **e**vidence **a**ppearing **r**eal. Fear-based thoughts are negative thoughts that make us feel as though we are inadequate. They torment us and keep us stagnated. The enemy knows if we live in fear we cannot move forward. The greatest weapon the enemy of our soul uses is fear. Fear paralyzes us. Therefore, we must guard our minds against fear at all cost! When fearful thoughts come into our minds, we should negate them by injecting positive thoughts. We have been learning to do this through our affirmations.

Affirmations are a form of auto-suggestion. Auto-suggestion is a term that applies to all suggestions and all self-administered stimuli that reaches the mind through the five senses. It is simply self-suggestion. We can control our thoughts by repetitiously imprinting on our brains our self-suggestions. When we continue to build up our minds with our own suggestions, the subconscious will take them and adapt them to our lives. These self-suggestions will eventually produce energy that influences the subconscious mind. There are no thoughts, whether negative or positive, that can enter the subconscious mind without the aid of auto-suggestion. When we experience fear, unconsciously we have held on to fearful thoughts, causing them to take root. Instead of sitting back allowing negative thoughts to take root in our minds, we must reject them by feeding our minds with positive thoughts. The subconscious mind is like a fertile garden. Weeds will sprout in abundance unless seeds are sown to produce desirable crops. The seeds represent positive thoughts. Therefore, we must sow positive thoughts in our minds to insure that weeds will not flourish.

Even when we sow our seed of positive thoughts, we still need water (or emotions and feelings) to make our harvest grow. Unemotional words do not influence our subconscious mind. When you say your affirmations and prayers out loud, you must speak them with feeling. Mean what you say and your words will take root! You will not achieve your desired results until you learn how to stimulate your subconscious mind through thoughts or spoken words which have been infused with passion and belief. This requires constant practice. When you say your affirmations, visualize yourself as accomplishing the mission you recite in your mind. When you believe by faith, you will receive your desired outcome. Over time, you will get better at producing results by consistently reciting your affirmations. The more you recite them, the more your desires will increase to a burning obsession. This obsession will create a major change within. You will wake up feeling energized and ready to conquer. This energy will bring your dreams to life!

Every successful person has confidence in themselves and their abilities. In order to become empowered, we must make personal confidence a habit or a lifestyle. Confidence is a combination of a positive attitude mixed with positive actions. Every day we can make a choice to have an attitude of gratitude and to think positively about ourselves and others. This attitude opens the doors of opportunity within us, which ultimately draws others to embrace our positive attributes.

Faith in ourselves is self-confidence. Without this attribute we are destined to fail. Each of us must make an effort to improve the way we feel about "self." As we accomplish positive goals and change our thinking, it will become easier to believe in ourselves. At the end of your day, take time to meditate on the things you did well that day. Congratulate yourself, and show yourself appreciation. Record the goals you accomplish and ponder on them. As you watch yourself improve and accomplish what you never imagined you could do, you will automatically increase your self-confidence. Do something special for yourself each week that you accomplish your goals. Remember, true happiness comes from within. As you make yourself happy, life will become more enjoyable. During rough times, think about your accomplishments. It is this positive energy that will keep you motivated to succeed. Confidence is the foundation you need to hold everything together, especially when times get rocky. In the past, many of us have allowed our confidence to be controlled by people and circumstances; today, we can take back that control! Do you want back your passion and desire, the longing you need deep down inside to push forward? Do you want back your faith, the ability to believe you can and will achieve your dreams? Do you want back your confidence, the foundation that holds you together when times get tough?

If so, let's turn to our Partner for assistance to restore ourselves. Let's pray: *"God, we thank You for revealing the power of desire, faith, and self-confidence. We now understand we need these attributes to reach our dreams in life. We ask that*

You stir up the desire and inner longing we need to accomplish our purpose and to achieve our goals. We ask that You reignite the childlike faith we once had. Give us the strength to believe that You will help us achieve all our dreams that align with Your will. We ask that You empower us to regain confidence in "self." Give us the ability to realize our potential within. Show us our strengths and reveal to us our gifts and talents. Allow us to excel and to reach heights we never imagined possible. We receive these answers now, as we harmoniously ignite our faith and desire to believe. Amen."

Wow! We are well on our way to empowerment! Let's close this chapter with an affirmation that will keep us focused on our mission: *"Today is a new day. Today I stand equipped to overcome. Today I have a deep-rooted desire to achieve all my dreams. I also have the faith I need to believe, so my dreams will come to pass. I am confident in myself. I am God's wonderful creation. He is my Partner so I know I can do all things. There is no barrier, no obstacle, no person and no situation that can stop me. If God is for me, then no man can successfully stand against me. Today I have arrived. I hold my dreams in my hands. I see myself in the place I want to be, so it is only a matter of time until my desired results will come to pass. I am indeed successful."*

CHAPTER QUESTIONS

1) What is desire?
2) What is faith?
3) What is self-confidence?
4) Why will you fail if you don't possess: a) desire, b) faith, and c) self-confidence?
5) How can you work on improving your: a) desire, b) faith, and c) self-confidence?

WRITING ASSIGNMENT

Create your own affirmation using the format below:

Today I have increased my desire. Desire is (fill in your answer). Today I have increased my faith. Faith is (fill in your answer). Today I have self confidence. I believe I can (fill in your answer). Daily I will increase my faith by (fill in the answer). Daily I will work on my self-confidence by (fill in the answer).

I am successful! I will achieve all of my dreams by using this affirmation daily until my dreams become my reality!

CHAPTER 8

The Power of Specialized Knowledge Skills

In our journey to empowerment, we have created a solid foundation to achieve our dreams. We understand the importance of purpose, we've ascertained our goals, we've created a partnership with our Higher Power, we've developed strategies to establish positive thinking and a positive attitude, we've learned how to develop good habits, and we've learned how to increase our desire and faith. Now we will learn about the power of developing specialized knowledge and skills.

This book has emphasized that we possess the ability to achieve our dreams. However, it's important not to downplay the fact that we are now labeled "ex-felons" or "ex-convicts." These titles have a negative stigma. We are looked at in society as the "lowest of the lowest," the "bottom of the barrel." This does not mean we cannot succeed, it just means that we will have to work that much harder to overcome this barrier. We have to equip ourselves to triumph. We do so by obtaining specialized knowledge and developing special skill sets in our desired field of interest. Unlike others, we cannot be mediocre in our performance and skills. We have to go over and above the call of duty to prove ourselves worthy. Don't worry, you won't be cheated out of anything! It is hard work and ambition that makes the difference between being average or extremely successful. We must return back to society programmed to over-achieve. It is the deep-rooted desire and determination to overcome our barriers that will push us to achieve what many others can't.

In Chapter 1, we talked about learning from our past, then letting it go. It is the lessons we've learned and the hardships that we've endured that actually give us an advantage over others. It is like a child whose mother tells her, "Don't put your hand on the stove, it will burn you." But the child is so intrigued by the fire that she doesn't listen and puts her hand on the stove and burns herself badly. The mother rushes her to the hospital where she is treated, bandaged and sent home. The little girl heals, but she still has scars on her hands. These scars forever remind her of the powerful flames of the fire. Just like this little girl, we possess the scars that came from the adverse actions of our past. Others who have not been hurt by the fire will continue to play with the flames. The girl, who has the visible scars as a reminder of her action, carefully avoids the fire. Those scars discipline and remind her of the consequences of her actions. Like this little girl, we possess the scars that remind us that we cannot do the same old things and expect different results. Let's take heed to this lesson!

In this chapter, I will outline for you a road map of actions you can follow that will lead you to success. If you implement these strategies in your plans and goals, you are sure to succeed. Remember, in order to be successful and to sustain it, you will have to work hard. There are no shortcuts, but the benefits far exceed the sacrifices. Be attentive. Review the strategies, and determine which will work best for you.

In order to excel, you must obtain wisdom and knowledge. Knowledge is the "what to do" and wisdom is the "how to do it." In every adventure we explore, we need these two ingredients to succeed. Without them, failure is guaranteed. Incarceration gives us the time we need to increase our knowledge. The first step to achieving your dreams is to read books about what you want to do, and books about others who have achieved their dreams. This is a vital prerequisite to achieving your success. You must become a master in your field or trade. If you are not interested in reading about the profession of your choice, take that as a sign that this may not be the field you are interested in pursuing. When you tap into your purpose and find the subject you are truly passionate about, you can spend hours reading about it, effortlessly. It will stir up desire in you and keep you motivated to achieve your dream. You can locate many useful books at the library, or you can have family members or friends go on to the Amazon or Barnes and Noble websites to purchase books for you. At these sites, they can type into the search engine the topic you wish to read about, and many references will come up. Each book will have a customer rating and a brief review that will help determine which selection will best fit your needs. As you read, you will gain the knowledge you need to develop your skill set in your desired occupational field. Don't just stop at reading a book or two. As long as you are in your field, continue to read books or other published materials written by the top authorities in your profession. They will give you many tips about the best way to achieve your dreams. You will be amazed how reading can help you become one of the best in your industry. You will have an advantage over the many others who don't take the time to investigate these avenues of information.

The *Voice of Consequences Enrichment Series* started out as an idea in my mind. My desire to accomplish it was based on my inner desire to obtain true reformation, but I wasn't sure about the way to accomplish my dream. One of the girls in my prison dorm let me borrow her copy of *Dan Poynter's Guide to Self-Publishing*. I read and passionately studied this book for weeks. I also read as many self-help books as I could get my hands on. I studied the techniques and strategies of these authors and combined them with my own strategies. Then, I tested them out on other inmates and myself, and I established that they work! My desire grew from my condition and circumstances, along with the empathy I had developed for the women around me. My passion was strong, but it still was not enough. Without the specialized knowledge I obtained from the books I have read, along with the faith I have received from reading my Bible daily, the *Voices of Consequences Enrichment Series* would not have been possible. I share my testimony because I am no different from you. If I can achieve, so can you! Start by making reading a priority in your life. Many things that you wish to know about life and how to achieve your dreams are already written. You just have to do the legwork to find the information. Instead of only dreaming about something, make it a reality! Find out how others obtained the same goal you desire. Reading is fundamental because it gives you the knowledge you need to succeed. Applied knowledge is true power. It will make you stand out from amongst the rest!

Another way to gain knowledge about a particular subject is to use the internet search engines. Over the years the internet has become the best source to find details on any topic or person. Simply go to Google.com, Yahoo.com or any other search engine on the net, type the topic in that you want to research and information will pop up, including books and articles that can offer you more information. Before you pursue any career, or choose an employer, do your research. Make sure this is indeed what you want to do and where you want to work.

After you determine through research that this is indeed the goal you wish to accomplish, find three people in your local area who are already successful in that field. You can find them in the telephone book, by word of mouth or even on the internet.

Reach out to them through phone, correspondence or in person. Let them know that you admire their success, and you are interested in reaching the same goal. Then, ask them if they will answer a few questions about how they achieved their success. This may seem frightening at first, but you will be surprised to see how many people are honored that someone else recognizes their hard work and wants to be like them. If they refuse to assist you, move on to the next person.

Make sure you are prepared in advance to ask all the questions that you would like answered. Prior to your approach, write down a list of questions. Some good questions to ask are listed below:

1) How did you get involved in your profession?
2) How much training did it require?
3) Where did you go to school for your training?
4) What are the perks about this profession?
5) What are some of your common struggles in this field?
6) How do you suggest I go about becoming proficient in this field?
7) Do you know of any good intern opportunities where I can volunteer my time to learn more about this field?
8) Can I reach out to you in the future to keep you abreast of my progress or call you if I have further questions?

The answers to these questions will give you the necessary insight on how you can achieve your goals. They may also help you to develop a relationship with someone who is already successful in your desired occupational field. Before you approach your new potential mentor, make sure that you are well informed about this profession. Your knowledge of the field will be the key ingredient that sparks this person's interest in assisting you. Read several books on the topic, and be prepared to answer questions they may ask you.

There are two types of knowledge you can obtain. One is general knowledge; the other is specialized knowledge. General knowledge consists of a variety of different topics but does not place emphasis on a particular subject matter. We obtain general knowledge in school, in our everyday functions, and from our interactions with others. Specialized knowledge consists of a particular field of studies or interest. It is this knowledge that enables you to become an expert in your field. Specialized knowledge includes subjects such as working as a beautician, in the culinary arts, as a plumber, social worker or accountant. In order to master a particular trade, you need to gain specialized knowledge in that field.

You can develop the skill sets you need in a particular field by going to college or a trade school. There are many specialized training programs and courses you can enroll in, even in prison. Each state has a certain allotment of money to help pay for education for ex-felons. Ask your counselor, probation or parole officer for information about this funding. You can also research on the internet what programs or resources are available in your area.

Many jails and prisons offer GED and college courses, as well as vocational training programs. Take advantage of them! Acquire as much knowledge that is available to you during your incarceration. It will lead to greater employment opportunities upon your release. Many resources and programs are offered in jails and prisons that you might not know about. Take a trip to the education or resource office in your prison and find out what's available. You will be surprised by how many untapped resources there are. All correctional facilities have an index to outside local outreach programs that provide housing, job training and placement, clothing and work stipends for released inmates. In order to get this information, you must request it!

Many colleges and training schools offer courses through correspondence so you can obtain a certificate or degree while you are incarcerated. You can use your time wisely and come out of imprisonment on top!

You can make it as an ex-felon. You can achieve your dreams and succeed. You can take this tragedy (or so you thought) and turn it into triumph, but it is up to you! Nobody is going to do the work for you. You must become educated, and you must learn the most you can about your desired profession. You must work hard to become successful. Do you truly want to succeed? If so, then follow me in this prayer: *"God, I thank You that You have given me the insight on what I must do to achieve my dreams. As my Partner I know You require me to do my part and You will do Yours. Today I vow to do my part. I will study, research and work diligently on becoming excellent in the profession I choose. Now I ask that You open doors of help and opportunity for me. I ask that You lead and direct me to the path of information and resources I will need. Help me to increase my wisdom, knowledge, and passion. Give me the instruments I need to possess my dreams. Amen."*

We are close to reaching our destination. This chapter has given many of us insight on our areas of weakness. A plan without the wisdom and knowledge to achieve it is useless. Now we must push up our sleeves and do our homework! That homework is ongoing research. It is up to each of us to discover the "how to" in accomplishing our dreams. No one can give this to you. You must create the opportunity for yourself through your own actions. The Bible states, in Matthew 7:7, the promise, "Ask, and it will be given to you; seek, and you will find; knock and it will be opened to you." Many people do not understand the true revelation behind this scripture. Ask means to go to your Partner and ask for what you want, but that alone doesn't insure you will get what you ask for. You still must do your part. Next, the scripture says to seek. To seek is to do your research, to study, to learn how you can become a better you. This is the step many misconstrue. Each of us must put in the work. No one will do it for us! Remember, seeking is a requirement for success. Once you seek you will be able to move onto the next step, which is to knock. To knock is to step up and ask for the opportunity. This is done only after you have done your research and preparation. These three steps provide the road map to your prosperity. There are no shortcuts! If you do your part, your Partner will have your back. Study and learn the specialized knowledge that you will need to excel. You now have the tools to take you to the top!

Let's close out the chapter with an affirmation that will keep us focused on doing the due diligence and research necessary to achieve our goals. *"Today is a new day. Today I have more power because I have gained knowledge. I know how to be successful. I must read, study and learn as much as I can about my area of interest. Each day I will take the necessary time to study the skills that will make me better equip. I will search passionately to find the best strategy for me to achieve my dreams. I will succeed because I will apply the knowledge I learn to my life. I am successful."*

CHAPTER QUESTIONS

1) What is general knowledge? What is specialized knowledge?
2) In which ways can you obtain specialized knowledge?

3) In which ways can you obtain general knowledge?
4) Why is specialized knowledge important?
5) How can you find someone to support you who is already successful in your desired occupational field?

WRITING ASSIGNMENT

Write down a plan of how you can develop specialized knowledge while imprisoned. Find the title of two books you can read that will teach you more about your desired profession. List the titles and the authors in your journal.

CHAPTER 9
The Power of Persistence and Focus

I n the last chapter we explored the importance of specialized knowledge. We learned how to expand our skill sets in specialized areas to excel and to overcome the barriers of being an ex-convict. We further explored the intense work ethic required to achieve success. In this chapter, we will discuss two main characteristics we must develop to obtain ultimate success, which are persistence and focus.

Persistence is the will power to continue despite opposition. Persistence is derived from our inner desire to achieve. Without persistence, it is impossible to succeed. Persistence requires inner strength, motivation and determination. These three factors create the energy of will power.

Focus is a concentrated effort of energy to accomplish a given task. It is the determination to concentrate on one subject at a time. Focus gives us the ability not to become sidetracked or distracted. It is concentrated effort that helps us achieve our accomplishments.

As we pursue our dreams, we must overcome many obstacles. To scale these barriers, it is important that we develop persistence and focus. It's time to develop a made-up mind, determined that nothing and no one will stop us from achieving our dreams. When you have a burning desire to achieve, it will create the will power or persistence you require to keep going, regardless of what vicissitudes stand in your way.

In Chapter 5, we talked about the power of developing good habits. In order to accomplish our mission, we need to develop the skill of persistence and make it a habit. When persistence becomes a part of our daily lifestyle, nothing will be impossible! Those who cultivate the habit of persistence create a shield around them as an insurance against failure. It is a wall that blocks the bumps and bruises of life. No matter how many times they seem to be defeated, they continue on. People who are always persistent eventually arrive at the top of the ladder of success. To these people, persistence becomes a state of mind. It is embedded deeply within them. They have an attitude that cries out: "I'm determined to make it. I refuse to lose." It is this inner strength that takes them everywhere in life they wish to go.

Many times we start projects off enthusiastically, ready to conquer the world! Then somewhere halfway through our mission we lose our focus and our drive, perhaps after encountering an obstacle, and we quit. Many of us have quit projects that would have brought us great joy had we pursued them just a little further and completed the task. An example of this character flaw is exhibited in the following example:

There were two girls who grew up together in a housing project in Jamaica Queens, New York. They were best friends for many years. The eldest friend was named Zena and the youngest was named Tameka. Tameka looked up to Zena and admired her style and abilities. Zena had a unique talent of taking old clothes and redesigning them into hot, new outfits. Tameka studied and watched Zena's techniques. Eventually, she also learned how to design clothes. After high school both girls decided to create a company called "Creative Stylez by Z&T." They were passionate about overcoming the obstacles of poverty and making it out of the ghetto. They used this passion to achieve success. The girls started off making trendy clothes for the people in there neighborhood. Their acclaim quickly spread, and they opened up a booth inside the Coliseum Mall in Jamaica Queens. Everyone from everywhere came to buy their clothes, even celebrities. Everything was great, until a couple of years went by and the business fell into a slump. During this time, it was hard for the girls to pay their bills. Zena wanted to quit. She had met a good man while being a part of this hot, new company, and she wanted to settle down with him. Although she was the main designer of the company, she was tired of the demands and long hours that the business required. Tameka on the other hand wanted to press on. After several struggles, during a phone conversation with Tameka, Zena terminated her position as a partner. She told Tameka she was sorry but she could no longer continue on with the business, and she hung up the phone. The partnership was over, but Tameka wasn't finished. You see, Tameka refused to go back to that old housing project. She didn't have a man to support her like Zena did, so she decided to lean on God. Tameka went to church the Sunday after Zena left her and wept at the altar. The old Pastor saw her tears and he embraced her. "God said He is here today to comfort you. He sees all that you have endured. He made you to be the winner that you are. Don't give up. Help is on the way," the Pastor said passionately as he held Tameka in his arms. The words of the pastor strengthened Tameka and gave her the desire to push forward. Tameka quickly regained her desire to achieve. She kept those words hidden in her heart.

Tameka held on to the store and relied on her own talent to make new creations. She changed the name of the company to, "Creative Creations by T.G." Tameka gained a new faithful Partner, Who knows all things and guarantees success—God. She stayed energized and creative. One day she came up with a new style of sweaters that were so unique their popularity *spread rapidly. With the money Tameka made she was able to open a store in Brooklyn and another store in Harlem. Everyone from everywhere began to compliment and rave about her extremely creative styles. One of the buyers for Macy's Department Store loved her sweaters so much that she offered Tameka a distribution deal to place her clothes in stores throughout the world. Today Tameka is no longer financially challenged; she has became a multi-millionaire, and an elite, recognized designer in her field.*

After achieving her success, one day she got a call from Zena. "Hey girl, how are you? I miss you so much. Congratulations. I see all you have done with our company. Things are not quite working out with me and Bill. Since I had the baby, he seems distant. So I was thinking, I should come back to New York. I have some great new ideas that can take our company to the top," Zena said with enthusiasm. Tameka paused and explained that she was helping a customer. She wrote down Zena's new number, and she hung up.

I want you to take a moment to think about what you would have done if you were in Tameka's situation? Would you call Zena back and give her another chance? Or, would you decide to reject her offer?

Many of us represent the Zenas of the world - smart people, with a lot of talent but lacking the focus and persistence to make our lives a success. If Zena would have held on just a little longer, she would have become a millionaire too! Tameka's focus was on success. Zena's focus started on success, but she let her love for a man take her focus elsewhere. Tameka experienced many obstacles, but she learned to take God on as a Partner. This allowed her the extra push she needed to make it. This is a good example of the power of persistence and focus. Tough times will come, so expect them, but they won't last. It's only a test! God never gives us gifts without first testing us. He wants to see if you really want success. He wants to see how committed you are to it and to what length you will go to maintain it. When you pass these tests and stand, when others quit, you are sure to be rewarded. Do you have what it takes to take a licking and keep on ticking? If you do, you will reap great rewards.

We sustain our persistence through operating in our purpose, which creates a burning desire within to achieve. We take our written statement of personal achievement and memorize it, holding it tightly in our hearts. Then, we live and breathe our purpose, allowing it to become one with us. We visualize ourselves in the place we want to be. As we visualize our success, we experience the feelings that come with this pleasure. This helps to build a wall in our minds that repels all negativity and discouraging influences. We also align ourselves strategically with those who support and encourage us in our mission. When we take these steps, we prepare ourselves to embark upon the voyage to our greatest victory.

In order to stay focused on our mission, we must create boundaries. Boundaries discipline us to stay within certain realms. When people and things don't line up with our purpose we quickly detach ourselves. When approached with a proposition, always ask yourself: "Will this help me achieve my purpose?" If not, ask yourself: "Will this delay my purpose?" It's good to be helpful and friendly, but make sure your assistance to others doesn't have a negative effect on your life. When offered a proposition that is not beneficial to you, ask yourself: "Is there anyone else who can do this task?" Evaluate what you are concentrating your efforts on. If you have something more important to do, see if someone else could perform this task. There will be tasks that you will need to take care of yourself, but which may be delayed. We have to learn how to prioritize the tasks that are beneficial to our growth. Choices or opportunities may arise that are very important and require your immediate attention. Don't procrastinate; get those things accomplished right away! The longer you allow them to pile up, the more dread you will feel about doing them.

It is important that we learn how to stay focused and not let distractions hinder us. Telephones, television, and other electronic devices are three major distractions that can weaken our focus. Be mindful of their power to distract us. When you have to stay focused to accomplish a certain task, turn these instruments off, so you can focus your full attention on what you are doing. Be mindful of other distractions that delay your productivity. As you recognize these distractions, be sure to uproot them.

Now that we have addressed the power of persistence and focus, and we have discussed possible obstacles, hindrances and distractions, let's talk about the struggles we may encounter in obtaining employment as an ex-convict. I want you to be equipped to overcome this hurdle. You become equipped by preparing yourself in advance with the strategies you will use to overcome this dilemma.

In the last chapter, I mentioned to you the scripture in Matthew 7:7; "Ask, and it will be given to you; seek, and you will find; knock, and it will be opened to you." We also discussed how to seek. Now, we will learn the art of knocking. After you have equipped yourself with the specialized knowledge you need to succeed in your field of choice, you must stand up and knock to receive the opportunity. Many people fear this task because they don't like rejection. You cannot take a "no" personally. It is simply a signal that this person is not ready for you, and that God has something else greater for you. If you are rejected, it's okay. Dust yourself off and knock again!

Think about how as children we had no problem knocking on the doors of strangers' homes on Halloween to receive candy. There were many people who denied us, but that didn't stop us! We didn't care about the strange lady who turned the lights out and hid behind the door. She didn't hinder or stop our mission; we simply moved on to the next house, and we moved eagerly with excitement. That's the same attitude we have to have when it comes to obtaining employment. Refuse to give up! Once you stand up and knock, your Partner will see to it that the right door of opportunity is opened.

With the negative stigma of being an ex-convict, when we knock we've got to come prepared. I'm going to share seven tips from Napoleon Hill's *Think and Grow Rich,* which you can use as assistance to get the job you desire.

STEPS TO GETTING THE EXACT POSITION YOU DESIRE:
1) Decide exactly what kind of job you want. If the job doesn't already exist, perhaps you can create it.
2) Choose the company or individual for whom you wish to work.
3) Study your perspective employer as to policies, personnel and chances of advancement.
4) By an analysis of yourself, your talents and capabilities, decide what you can offer and plan ways and means of showing advantages, services, development, and ideas that you believe you can do successfully.
5) Forget about "a job." Forget whether or not there is an opening. Forget the usual routine of "Have you got a job for me?" Concentrate on what you can give.
6) Once you have your plan in mind, arrange with an experienced writer to put your ideas on paper in a neat form, and in full detail.

7) Present this to the proper person with authority and he will do the rest. Every company is looking for people who can give something of value, whether it is ideas, services or "connections."

I share these tips with you because I want you to start thinking outside the box. Stop looking for what's available and concentrate on what you want to do. If you desire a particular job, you will have that much more passion to obtain it. Even if you are not presently qualified, be willing to intern or take a low paying position to get where you want to go. Once you are in the company, you can work hard to prove yourself. Hard work always pays off; you will be recognized, and after recognition comes promotion. Be willing to sweep floors and clean desks. Don't work with an attitude, do your job with pride because you have a plan—climbing the ladder of success.

I'll share a story with you about a public figure we all know. He grew up in Mount Vernon, New York and had aspired to be in the music industry. This young man graduated high school and went on to attend Howard University. He was so focused and persistent with his dream that he began to promote parties, while he interned at Uptown Records and attended school full-time. He would travel from Washington, DC to New York on a regular basis to intern at Uptown Records. He worked hard, without receiving a paycheck, but he had a plan. All he wanted to do was to get his foot in the door and prove himself, and he did just that! He went on to obtain a paying job at the company, and later he departed and started his own record label, called Bad Boy Records. This man's name is Sean "P-Diddy" Combs. Today he is very successful, selling millions of records worldwide. Why was he able to achieve such grand success? He was focused, persistent and passionate about his mission. He would not take "no" for an answer, and neither should we! Knock, knock, knock! If that doesn't work, knock again! That's the only way you will succeed!

One of the biggest hurdles is getting an employer to hire you after he finds out that you are an ex-convict. We combat this issue by explaining our past dilemmas and having the ability to sell ourselves. The key to gaining employment is to show the employer you are ready for the job and have the necessary qualifications. Set forth your qualities and let him or her know you are up for the challenge. Then explain that you are an ex-felon and you know because of your background you will have to work harder to prove yourself.

Each state has benefits for employers who hire ex-felons. These may include tax breaks and financial incentives. There is bonding you can obtain as an ex-felon that will protect the employer if something goes wrong. Know these preventive measures and the perks offered to your employer for hiring you. Sell the advantages to your future employer. Also, be willing to take a lower position and work your way up. And if necessary, intern part-time and prove yourself. Your drive, ambition and dedication will move the employer to give you a chance. Show that you are well-educated on all facets of your desired position and about the company where you are applying. Use your knowledge and wit to win your employer over. Explain the work and due diligence you have done to correct your life. Let the employer know how dedicated you are to accomplishing your mission. Passion moves people! Utilize your passion to make your employer believe in you.

Come to your job interview early. This is important because it shows your future employer that you are dependable. Dress to impress. Make sure your clothes are clean and well-pressed, and more importantly, respectful. No thighs or cleavage showing. Stick to dark colors, i.e. navy, black or gray slacks or skirts and a crisp white top or blouse. Make eye contact with the interviewer. Be pleasant and smile. Shake hands firmly when introduced and when the meeting is over. The key to your success is the ability to sell yourself and your services; when asked questions about your desired position, claim the position by saying things like "When I'm employed by your company I will...," and "When I greet the customers here I will...." This tactic will convince your potential employer you have confidence that you will gain the position. Employers like to see employees with self-confidence. Therefore, claim your position during the interview. When asked about your goals, let your interviewer know you are looking for long-term employment in his or her company. Your goal is to reach the top heights in this profession. Employers usually get turned off by overly-motivated people. They believe such people will use their job as a stepping stool, then leave. Make sure you express your desire to stay and grow within the company. After the interview, follow up with a thank you letter. Thank the interviewer for their time, and again express your confidence by stating you anticipate hearing from them and you look forward to working with their company.

Succeeding after prison won't be easy, but it's not impossible. With hard work and effort you can do it! Are you ready to climb up that grand ladder called success? If, so, let's get some help from our Partner. Let's pray: *"God, I thank You for revealing to me the power of focus and perseverance. These are the characteristics I need to possess my dreams. I'm ready and willing to commit my time, dedication and devotion. Now I ask You to strengthen me and help me to increase my persistence and my focus. When I'm ready to knock, I ask that You lead me to the correct doors to knock on.*

Touch the hearts of the people whom I will need to assist me in becoming a better person. Extend new opportunities to me. Give me the ability to not take rejection personally but rather to use it as a springboard to get my desired answer—'yes.' Amen."

Wow! We are almost at the end of our journey. We now possess most of the tools we need to complete our mission. It's key that we acknowledge daily the importance of focus and persistence. As we do so, our days will become much more productive. Let's use this affirmation to keep us locked in on our mark: *"Today is a new day. I am empowered today because I understand the need to activate my persistence and my focus. I will hold firmly to my desires with a burning passion. This passion will create great persistence and drive within me. I will stay focused and plan my day accordingly. I will analyze the tasks that come before me. I will decide what I will do, what I will defer, what I will delegate to others, and what I will not do. My decisions will determine my effectiveness. I will not let distractions take me away from my mark. I will persistently stay focused. I will achieve all my goals. I am successful."*

CHAPTER QUESTIONS

1) What is persistence? What is focus?
2) What are boundaries? Why are they necessary?
3) What steps do we need to take to succeed in our desired occupation?
4) What are some key strategies to gaining employment?
5) What techniques can we utilize to maintain our persistence and focus?

WRITING ASSIGNMENT

Write down a list of actions you can take to daily increase your persistence and focus. Write a letter to a future employer and explain to him the reasons why he/she should hire you for the position you desire. Elaborate on this position in detail (a position made based on your inner desires) and outline your qualifications. Also mention key points about the company that you've learned through your research. (Include points that are important to you about your prospective employer.)

CHAPTER 10
The Power of Love and Generosity

O n our journey to achieving our dreams, we have learned about many different attributes we must possess to become successful. We've discussed in detail the attributes of desire and faith, as well as persistence and focus. Along with these, there are two more key characteristics we must possess: love and generosity. Without these two characteristics, we will be unable to sustain success. In this chapter, we will explore the power of love and generosity and learn the true definition of each. We will also explore their positive effects on our lives, as well as the negative consequences that result when we lack them.

Love is a term that many of us use loosely and incorrectly. We meet a new person, and we quickly say, "I love you." Or, we pass through the mall and see a pair of nice shoes we like, and we say, "I love them." Some of us are in jail because someone told us, "I love you," and we believed them. We did things they advised us to do, and we lived our lives to please them. In the end, we discovered their love wasn't really love at all.

We live in a "self-centered" world. Most people are concerned only about themselves. They aren't interested in things that don't benefit them. Life for many is a race to see who will reach the finish line first. Like crabs in a basket, many are willing to do whatever it takes to get to the top, including pulling down others to get there faster. Many of us have participated in this rage. We have manipulated others into giving us what we want. We backbit, we back-stabbed, lied and cheated our way up what we perceived was the ladder to success. Some of us even arrived at our destination, only to discover that our shortcut was actually the long, and wrong, route. Now we are left to begin again. Think about it. Many of us are incarcerated for crimes that brought us financial gain. We drove luxury cars, lived in expensive homes; we wore the finest clothes and ate well each day. At one point our way of life seemed good, until the big bang of imprisonment hit. Many of us were shocked how quickly the fruits of our labor disappeared. The things we worked so hard to have were taken in the blink of an eye. What a hurtful feeling! Now as we reflect back, we begin to ask ourselves: Was it worth it? Of course not! We could have reached the top with integrity. Had we done so, we would be enjoying the fruits of our labor, instead of being incarcerated.

There are many varieties of love. Lets explore love from God's perspective. The Bible states, in I Corinthians 13:4-7, "Love suffers long and is kind, love does not envy; love does not parade itself, is not puffed up, does not behave rudely, does not seek its own, is not provoked, thinks no evil, does not rejoice in iniquity, but rejoices in the truth; bears all things, endures all things."

According to this scripture, love is unconditional. It is not based on what another does. It is an inner feeling of joy, peace, adoration and appreciation for all of God's creations. Love also expresses appreciation to our Creator for all His wonderful works. We honor God when we love all mankind as we love ourselves.

Love has no barriers. It recognizes the good in all mankind, regardless of their faults. It deliberately recognizes the good and discards the bad. Love is not selfish. It looks for ways to embrace others in need. It is not turned off even when others spitefully misuse us. Even then, love continues to radiate; yet it takes care of the one who expresses it. Love rejoices in the victories of others regardless of the current state of the one who is expressing this love. It lifts up those who are down and doesn't try to overshadow others for its own gain. Love is kind and gentle. It's never rude. When others are hostile and nasty, love recognizes the circumstances behind their anger. Love responds with kindness, mercy and compassion, piercing the heart of the one who was rude. Love is powerful. It is the secret ingredient that initiates change. Evil cannot exist where love is stirred up. It eventually has to dissipate. We win each battle when we use love as our weapon. Love has the power to make our enemies into our friends.

"Why should I love, when no one is returning my love," is a common question many of us ask ourselves. But, we always benefit when we love others. It is God Who rewards us, not man. We offer our love as a sacrifice and an expression of honor to our Creator. As we begin to base our lives on true love, we create a powerful energy that stirs up the universe and brings us back multiple expressions of love and blessings. We can't reap what we have not yet sown. Start planting today and spread love. Watch the abundant harvest that will come your way!

Everything that is successful is built with love. When we selflessly care about others, we tap into purpose. Purpose fulfills us, which makes work pleasurable and easy. When we enjoy what we do, we share that energy with those we are helping. They feel our expression of love, which ultimately assists them in their own journey. This seed of positivity is very powerful. It creates a chain of energy that attracts others to join its force. It is the reason we were created - to be God's wonderful expressions of love.

When we bring love into our profession, it causes others to be attracted to us. Everyone wants to be loved and honored. When we show love and gratitude to people they want to express it back. Love brings about promotion in the marketplace. It also causes a customer base to grow. Everyone wants to do business with people who they feel appreciate them. In order to be successful, you must perform your duties with love. Love is what produces excellent performance, which will be noted, recognized and ultimately honored with promotion. Let's explore together an example of the power of love:

Michelle grew up in the inner city of Detroit, Michigan. She was raised in a rough area and quickly adapted to her environment. Michelle was the oldest of her four brothers and two sisters. Michelle's mom was a single mother who struggled to make ends meet. Michelle was very tall and beautiful. She had the stature of a model, but her dream as a young child was to become a nurse. By the time Michelle was fifteen, she was highly sought-after by many of the boys in her neighborhood. They would ask her out on dates and shower her with gifts. When Michelle was sixteen she met a twenty-three-year-old drug dealer named Bobby. Bobby became Michelle's boyfriend. He showered her with fine gifts and even took care of her family. Bobby's money won over Michelle's mom. Fascinated with his wealth and affluence, Michelle's mother allowed Bobby to move in with the family. Bobby became the head of Michelle's household. At first, life with Bobby seemed great. Michelle believed she'd found true love as well as a solution to her family's troubles. Bobby viewed Michelle as a trophy with benefits. His benefits included having Michelle any way he wanted her and the use of Michelle's house as a spot to store his drugs. Over time, as Bobby began to show a lack of respect for Michelle and her family, the house graduated from the stash spot to the house where Bobby sold his drugs. Bobby also lured Michelle and her mother into selling drugs for him from their home. The money enticed them, so they both agreed. The house became the new, "hot spot" and over time Bobby was there less often. He became consumed with using the same tactics to lure in the next "victim," another poor, pretty girl from the neighborhood.

Shortly thereafter, Michelle's house was raided, and Michelle and her mom were both apprehended by the Feds. They were locked up with no bail, but they refused to give Bobby up. Michelle's mom convinced Michelle to take the charges so she could go free. Her rationale was that one of them needed to be there for the other kids in the house, so Michelle agreed. She took the rap for Bobby and her mom.

After being locked up, she discovered she was pregnant. Pregnant and in jail, Michelle faced up to 20 years. She reached out to Bobby, who refused to accept her calls. Lonely and abandoned, Michelle sought her Higher Power. She began to go to Islamic studies classes inside the county jail and surrendered her wretched life over to God.

Several months passed and Michelle was in her third trimester of pregnancy. With still no clue of her fate, she began to find the joy and beauty in each day. One day a girl who was also pregnant, came into the facility where Michelle was housed. Like Michelle's, her home was raided for drugs. The other girls in the pod began talking about the new girl's case when they read about her arrest in the local newspaper. Michelle's curiosity led her to read the article. In shock, she discovered Bobby was apprehended inside this girl's house, and the newspaper stated this girl was also expecting Bobby's baby. The article was entitled "King Pin Down." It talked about all of the areas in Detroit that Bobby had control over and all the females he used as his mules to stash, to carry, and to sell drugs for him.

Over time Michelle and the girl became friends. They both mourned their negligence and naiveté about Bobby's scheme. Michelle stood before a federal judge for sentencing two weeks before her baby was due. The prosecutor and federal agents *were very compassionate toward Michelle. They knew from their investigation she was swindled into this lifestyle by Bobby, along with his many other girls, so they showed Michelle mercy. She received a 24-month sentence, of which she had already served eight months. She was sentenced to go to a program that allowed her to keep her child with her for a year. That was just enough time for her to finish her sentence.*

Michelle was released from prison and decided to live life the right way. She temporarily received public assistance and went back to school. One day Michelle's daughter got sick, so she took her to the hospital. While they were in the E.R., she met a volunteer who worked inside the hospital. The volunteer approached Michelle and her baby and treated them both with love and care. She made sure she got all the assistance she needed at the hospital and helped Michelle keep her miserable, crying child as comfortable as possible. This lady's genuine love sparked a flame in Michelle's heart. At that moment, she knew she wanted to offer others the same love she felt from this lady. She was amazed to learn that this lady wasn't a worker employed by the hospital; instead, the woman was a volunteer. This knowledge prompted Michelle to inquire how she could sign up to become a volunteer.

Michelle went to school full-time and volunteered at the hospital part-time for 15 hours each week. Michelle worked diligently at her position as a volunteer. She showed the same care and compassion she and her daughter had received. Michelle met a lot of people in a short time. Many of them kept in contact with her and offered love and support for her daughter. They bragged about Michelle's service to others. Eventually, she obtained a paid position at the hospital.

Four years later, Michelle completed parole with excellence, finished college and is now the Coordinator of Public Relations at the hospital, a position which pays close to six figures. Michelle didn't forget about the girls she met in prison; she helped several of them get jobs, including Bobby's other daughter's mother, whom she had met in jail. Michelle is happy. She is now engaged to one of the doctors at the facility and, more importantly, she is serving others and fulfilling her purpose.

What a story! How many parts of this story are similar to your own? Michelle had a rocky start but she changed her course for the better. Michelle thought she'd found love when she met Bobby, but to her bitter disappointment she discovered she was wrong. Bobby's false love almost ruined her life! Michelle's life changed when she took God on as her Partner. She didn't have to avenge herself. God did it for her! In jail Michelle found love and continued to express it. She did what most people wouldn't do. She worked for free as a volunteer, and her efforts paid off. Others recognized and embraced her love, and she was promoted. She didn't stop there; she also reached back and helped other girls coming out of prison. What a true act of love! Had she not been willing to give love a try, who knows what she would be doing today. She was even able to help Bobby's daughter's mother find a job. If you were Michelle, would you have done the same?

Now that we've explored the power of love, let's discuss the importance of generosity. Generosity is the selfless act of giving to others in need. Unlike love, which is an expression, generosity is the act of giving another something of value that you possess. One of the hardest things for many of us to share or give away is our money. Money is valuable to us, making it difficult to part with.

In order to maintain true success, we must not only be willing to offer our time and our service; we must also be willing to give our money.

When we offer a portion of the money we earn to charities, churches or others in need, we are ultimately showing God our gratitude. This is our way of saying, "Thank You for allowing me to be in a position to help someone less fortunate than myself." This sacrifice will make us feel as though we individually are making a difference. This act of service is part of fulfilling our purpose.

There is a universal law called the Law of Reciprocity. It states: the more you give, the more you will receive. Look at the lives of some of the richest people on Earth, such as Oprah Winfrey and Bill Gates. They both prove the truth of this law. They are among our world's generous philanthropist. The more they give, the more successful they become. You cannot expect to be blessed if you are selfish and hoard your earnings. As you spread your earnings with others, you ignite the universe to bring you more of what you have given away. Today, make a choice to be happy, fulfilled and successful. Make it a practice to give. Purposely set aside a part of your earnings to give back to those who are less fortunate than you. This is one of the greatest principles you can incorporate into your life. Watch how quickly generosity will come back to you in abundance!

Now that we understand the benefits of love and generosity, it is important to know the consequences if we don't incorporate these principles into our lives. If we don't share love, then we will not receive it. The opposite of love is hate. Hate comes with cruelty and torment. Whatever we sow is what we will reap back. If we are not generous to others, others won't be kind to us. Then, we will always remain in a state of lack. There are no exceptions to the rule! Many can gain without showing acts of love and generosity, but ultimately their gain will be lost. Love and generosity are the glue we need to sustain our prosperity.

Are you willing to open the doors of your heart to spread love and generosity? If so, let's say this prayer: *"God, I thank You for showing me the importance of love and generosity. I know I need these attributes in order to achieve my dreams and to sustain my blessings. Now I ask You to give me a heart that is designed to love and be a blessing. Grant me a deep-rooted compassion for others. Help me to see the good in everyone, in all situations. Allow me the ability to forgive those who mistreat me and wrongfully use me. Help me to understand the circumstances behind their actions, helping me to show mercy towards them. Enable me to show those who dislike me the same love I give to others. I now receive my new heart given to me by Your power. Amen."*

We are getting closer and closer to our mark of achievement. Let's close out this chapter with an affirmation to keep us focused on the power of love and generosity. *"Today marks a brand new day. Today I possess the attributes of love and generosity in my heart. Today I can make it because love is my shield and generosity is my sword. I will use these two weapons to overcome all barriers. I will look at all things and all people with love in my heart. I will greet everyone with my love. I will love my enemies, and they will become my friends. I will love my friends, and they will become my family. I will recognize the good in everyone regardless of their faults, and eventually I will tear down the walls of hate that surround them. While loving others, I will be sure to love myself. I will do good works and act as a loving person. I will not allow myself to be inflicted with the malice of others. I will detach from those who try to misuse me, and love them from a distance. I will love others as I love myself. I will use generosity to make many friends. I will give my best to others in need. When people and things displease me, I will ask myself: "What can I give?" When I give, my actions will create change in the hearts of those to whom I express my generosity. I will break down the walls of their reluctance and hate by my gifts of generosity. I now understand my power. I am empowered with a heart full of love and generosity."*

CHAPTER QUESTIONS

1) What is love?
2) What is generosity?
3) What acts are sometimes misconstrued as love? Why?
4) What did Bobby do that was misconstrued by Michelle as love?
5) Why were the actions of the volunteer who helped Michelle so powerful?

WRITING ASSIGNMENT

Identify areas in your life where you can express love and generosity. Create a written well-organized plan of acts of love and generosity you will share with others. Start where you are right now and expand, in writing, your plan to include where you will be in the future.

CHAPTER 11

The Power of Enthusiasm and Balance

W e've learned a lot, and we're bringing our journey to a successful close. We now understand the "how to" strategies we need to implement in order to successfully achieve our goals. Additionally, we've explored the attributes we need to possess to overcome the stigma of being an ex-felon. Now it's time to learn how we can get to the finish line without burning out. In this chapter, we will discuss the importance of enthusiasm and balance in our lives. These two characteristics will help us to remain steady and to sustain our joy and happiness during our journey.

Enthusiasm is the outward expression of joy, gratitude and appreciation for what we do. It is our expression of motivation created by our deep desire and passion. When we are enthusiastic, we are motivated to achieve. Enthusiasm is necessary to perform with excellence. When you enjoy your job, others will enjoy your service. Enthusiasm is the key that opens the door to promotion.

Balance is the organized level of order in which we spend our time. Well-balanced use of time should include God, work, family and "self." These areas should represent our top priorities. Each area must receive the time and nurturing needed to develop. Each area relies on the other to mutually produce enjoyment and ultimate success. When we live life with balance, we become whole in every aspect of our lives.

Many people wake up dreading the day even before it starts. Work to them is a chore that they hate but need to do to pay their bills. Their dread is so deep within them that you can recognize it in their outward expressions. They are rude, nasty and short-tempered. You can also tell by their lack-luster performance that they dread what they do. These people lack enthusiasm.

When you have enthusiasm you wake up happy and expectant, eagerly anticipating the events each day holds. You go to work excited. Your joy is so deeply rooted that it's expressed in your greetings and service to others. Your happiness becomes contagious. You smile at the lady who started her day off with a negative attitude, and she has no choice but to smile back. Your spirit of enthusiasm is so powerful that it spreads to the hearts of others. By the end of the day everyone around you is happy, and they don't have a clue why.

Enthusiasm is a gift. Those who have it pass it on. They become the leaders and winners within their circles because everyone wants to be around them. We win in life when we maintain our enthusiasm. Enthusiasm may be difficult at times to create. Therefore, we each have to discover creative strategies that will help us develop and maintain our enthusiasm.

Instead of being uptight and serious, purposely make each task you do fun. For instance, if you have to go out on a delivery, turn your radio on in the car. Keep your favorite CD within reach. Pop it in and sing your way to your destination. This and other like strategies make the day go by faster and causes you to have more fun.

Maybe you have a task to perform, such as counting inventory or cleaning your work area. Do it while you hum a tune in your head. Don't be so serious. Make what you do fun. Challenge yourself. See how quickly and efficiently you can finish your task, and then try each day to beat your best time score.

Using various techniques such as these can make your day-to-day duties exciting. Challenge yourself so you don't become bored with your daily tasks.

It is important to take breaks throughout the day. Do not wear yourself out. During one of your breaks, use the time to meditate. Dump all the negative thoughts you've collected that day and visualize yourself accomplishing all your goals. This helps us to maintain enthusiasm. It reminds us there is purpose in what we do. It's all for a greater benefit—long-term success!

Balance is a major attribute that many people in our society lack. We often over-extend ourselves in one area and completely neglect another area. If we want to be successful, we must take time out for God, family, work and "self." Each of these areas is important. They must each receive our time and attention. The only way to ensure balance in our lives is to create a weekly schedule and stick to it. Let's explore a schedule example that demonstrates the proper balancing of time:

Martha gets up one hour earlier each day to spend time with God. She uses this time for prayer and reading God's Word. Then, she goes to work, Monday through Friday from 9 am - 5 pm. On Tuesdays and Thursdays she goes to the gym from 6 pm – 8 pm to work out. On Monday and Wednesday nights, she dedicates her time to her children. On Mondays, after she helps her children with homework, they choose a movie and watch it together. On Wednesdays they have family night and family Bible studies, where they hold a question-and-answer session. On Saturdays, Martha rests. She wakes up late and uses that day to organize her thoughts. Every Saturday night Martha goes out with her husband and drops the children off with her mom. This is her special time with her husband. On Sunday the family goes to church together along with Martha's mom. When they return from church, the family eats dinner together at her mother's house. Martha goes to bed early Sunday night to prepare for work on Monday.

Martha has managed to do what many others fail to do: She maintains a balance in her life. She is successful at her job. She is successful as a mother, daughter and wife. She is successful in fulfilling her obligations to God, and she is successful in caring for "self." Martha has tapped into wholeness. She has success in every aspect of her life. We can be just like Martha and enjoy this same kind of success. We achieve this by creating a schedule and maintaining balance.

Let's take a moment to explore another example of a woman who does not properly maintain a balance in her life. Pay close attention to the consequences she suffers in the example below:

Shaneeda lives in Philadelphia, PA. She was just released from spending two and a half years in state prison. Shaneeda has two children, five years old and eight years old. She is fortunate to have a loving mother and husband that help her maintain her household. Shaneeda is trying her best to do the right thing. She vows never to return to prison. This is Shaneeda's schedule: Each day she gets up and says a small prayer while brushing her teeth; she goes to work from 7 am – 3 pm, Monday through Friday. She then rushes to school from 4pm-8pm, Tuesday and Thursday. Monday, Wednesday and Friday she goes straight home, and she closes her door to study. By the time her husband gets home she is exhausted. She always kisses and hugs him, but she is too tired to perform her wifely duties. Shaneeda's children love her very much. She loves them, too. But, she spends little or no time with them because of her busy schedule. Every time Shaneeda's husband wants to spend time with her, she is either studying or doing work for her job. Shaneeda started going to church with the entire family every Sunday, but she stopped going to use that time to sleep. Shaneeda sleeps all day Sunday and on Monday gets up to repeat her schedule.

Does Shaneeda's schedule represent a balance? Can she maintain success with that kind of schedule? Let's find out as the story continues:

Shaneeda's schedule works out fine in the beginning; her mother and husband are both proud of her rehabilitation efforts. But her little children are growing older, and the oldest child, a girl, begins to act out in school. Shaneeda sends her mother to the school because she is too busy to go. At the meeting, her mom learns that the child told her teacher, "My mother doesn't love me." Worse, Shaneeda's husband, tired of the neglect he feels at home and unhappy with all the extra weight Shaneeda has gained, begins cheating on her with his new co-worker. Shaneeda accidentally discovers her husband's infidelity when she logs on to his computer to retrieve an address of their mutual friend. Shaneeda becomes heartbroken. Her grades begin to slip because she cannot concentrate. She also begins to slack off in her job, where she recently received a written warning. Shaneeda's life is in shambles!

Shaneeda must do something quick to keep things in order. What can Shaneeda do to change her course of life? Do you think she can turn around her mess? Miracles happen when we create balance. When life is out of order, we must stop, evaluate the path we have taken, and find a way to create an adequate balance in our lives. Let's explore how Shaneeda regains balance in her life.

Shaneeda and her husband met with the pastor of their church for marriage counseling. Shaneeda decided to give her husband another chance, after she contacted her husband's co-worker (whom she thought he was cheating with), at the parking lot of his job. She discovered they'd only flirted with each other and discussed an affair but never got a chance to carry it out. The pastor told Shaneeda she went wrong when she first neglected her time with God and then with her family. When Shaneeda first came home from prison, she was on fire for God. She was always at the church on time for services and also volunteered her help. Then, Shaneeda got the job she had been praying for and the money she needed to go to school. Slowly, Shaneeda abandoned God by getting caught up in the blessings she received. Shaneeda realized and acknowledged her faults. She repented, and so did her husband. They both worked out a schedule to maintain happiness in their lives. This is Shaneeda's new balanced schedule:

Monday through Friday, Shaneeda gets up a half hour early and reads her Bible and prays. Then, she heads off to work from 7 am – 3 pm. On Tuesdays and Thursdays she goes to school from 4 pm – 8 pm. On Wednesdays and Fridays she goes to the gym from 4 pm – 6 pm. Monday night is family night. She uses that time to play games and watch movies with her children. She makes sure she is the one to put the kids to sleep each night at 9 pm, and then she studies one hour each night from 9 pm – 10 pm. At 10 pm each night she recaps her day with her husband and falls asleep in his arms. Friday after work she picks up the kids, and she and her husband do something fun with them. Last week they went to Chuck E. Cheese's. On Saturday, Shaneeda catches up on sleep and relaxes with her husband. Saturday nights, the couple has alone time and usually goes out to eat. On Sunday the whole family goes to church and they come home to eat a home-cooked meal together.

Since Shaneeda has implemented this new schedule, she feels so much happier. Her husband, mother and children are happier too! She has now tapped into wholeness. She's successful at her job, she's a successful mother, wife and daughter, and *she's successfully fulfilling her obligations to God. Shaneeda feels happy inside, which can be seen and felt outwardly. She's finally achieved the true success she's been seeking! You and I are no different from Shaneeda; we can have the same successes, but we must live a balanced life.*

You also cannot maintain success without good health. We care for ourselves by watching the food we eat. It is unhealthy to eat fast food five days a week; we must eat nutritious meals. We must also exercise in order to maintain good health. There are many great benefits to physical fitness. Exercise helps us to live longer, enjoy great vitality and sustain a better quality of life. By exercising and watching our health, we will reap the rewards of long life and vitality as we grow older.

We don't have to over-exert ourselves. If you are already healthy and maintain a normal weight, you can exercise 20 minutes a day and receive fabulous results. One of the easiest ways to exercise is to walk around your block or area a few times each day. Studies show if you take a 45-minute walk, 4 times a week, you can lose up to 18 pounds over a year without dieting.

Exercise has many benefits. It helps you improve your sleeping habits, increases your energy levels, relieves stress and anxiety, protects against injury, promotes a healthy posture, relieves digestive disorders and enhances your self-image, which ultimately expands your life span.

To achieve the best results, we should exercise for at least 30 minutes each day, 5 days a week. This workout should include stretching. You can achieve this goal by playing a sport, doing aerobics, jogging or working out on an exercise bike or treadmill. There are many local gyms you can join. If you are financially able, you can even hire a personal trainer.

Exercise must become a habit. For long-term results and healthy living, make exercise your choice today.

Are you ready to become successful by living a balanced life? If so, let's pray: *"God, I thank You for making me aware of the importance of enthusiasm and balance. I know I will need these ingredients to maintain my success and happiness. Increase my knowledge of all the techniques I can use to maintain my enthusiasm. Help me to always keep a heart of gratitude and energy to back it up. Show me how to maintain balance in every area of my life. Awaken me when I begin to lose my balance, so I can quickly regroup. Teach me ways I can help keep my family, fellow workers and You happy. Help me to stay rooted and grounded in all that I do. Amen."*

We've gained so much wisdom in such a short period of time. Now let's say an affirmation to help us remember the importance of enthusiasm and balance: *"Today is a new, brighter day because I have learned the importance of enthusiasm and balance. Each day I will keep my flame of enthusiasm lit, and I will use it to get through my daily tasks. If my spirit becomes low, I will sing a song or think of a happy moment to rekindle my joy. I will remember all the things I have to be grateful for and keep my eyes focused on my future reward for my hard work. I promise to stick to my schedule and balance my time between God, my family, my work and myself. Therefore, I will achieve wholeness in every aspect of my life, and I will enjoy living!"*

CHAPTER QUESTIONS

1) What is enthusiasm?
2) What is balance?
3) Why are enthusiasm and balance important?
4) Why are exercising and eating healthy important?
5) What can we do to insure a balanced life?

WRITING ASSIGNMENT

Write down a plan of what you can do now to create enthusiasm and balance in your life. Make a weekly schedule reflecting a balanced lifestyle that you can put into action today.

CHAPTER 12

The Power of Perception

We have reached the last stop on our journey. We are now armed and equipped with all the tools and information we will need to achieve our dreams. We've learned to take the lessons we've acquired from our past mistakes, then let the past go. We've accepted the help of our "Higher Power" as our Partner. We've sharpened and developed our positive thinking skills. We've learned how to recognize and define our purpose. We've assessed our bad habits and replaced them with good habits. We learned how to turn our goals into an organized plan. We've learned how to tap into the power of desire and faith. We've learned strategies to develop our specialized knowledge and skills. We've adopted the principles of persistence and focus. We've tapped into the power of love and generosity, and we've explored the attributes of enthusiasm and balance. These new skill sets will help us establish a strong foundation if we apply them to our lives. Now it's time to explore the key ingredient that will help illuminate the attributes we've already learned, which will keep us grounded on the road to fulfilling our purpose. This attribute is the power of perception. We each hold all the power we need to achieve true success in the perception of our minds. We will explore the gift of perception and its attributes in this chapter.

We've learned in Chapter 4 that true success lies in finding our purpose. The world may label success and define it according to material gain, yet this isn't real success at all. A person can have more money and material items than anyone else in the world and still be miserable and unhappy. Success is wholeness, nothing missing, nothing broken, in every aspect of our lives, including health, family, finances, spirituality and self. If any of these areas are lacking, that imbalance will inevitably affect the whole. It is our goal in this journey to be fulfilled from the inside out, achieving true prosperity. This goal can be accomplished, but it will take time, diligence and patience. Our greatest challenge moving forward will be to recognize our growth and development. In order to grow, we must be challenged. Challenges come in the form of tests, trials and tribulations. Challenges often aren't fun. They exert our energy and at times give us the feeling of defeat. Today we must develop the skill set of perception; we must learn to see the opportunity that lies in each obstacle, so we can embrace it. Oftentimes when we experience challenges, we fight our hardest to avoid them. We shun them, and do whatever we can in order to divert them. Unfortunately, in many instances we block the very instruments that were sent to lead us to our purpose.

There is only one way to find our purpose. We have to go through obstacles. This means to experience the hurt, endure the pain, learn from the lessons and move on. Everyone in life must endure some hardships. They are the experiences that propel us into growth. For some of us, hardships are endured earlier on in life. For others, hardships occur later. The bottom line is, there is no way to avoid life's obstacles! Therefore, we must go through them. You cannot cross the bridge of life without riding through obstacles. When we understand and retain this truth, we begin to change our perception. Then, we no longer view our obstacles as crises. Instead, we perceive the opportunity that lies behind them. The gift of perception immediately decreases our pain and gives us the strength we need to overcome adversities. Our perception enables us to perform like diamond miners. When a diamond miner discovers the mountain where diamonds may exist, he knows in advance it's going to take a lot of work to extract the diamonds. Even when they are discovered, the diamonds will not be in their final form. It takes hard work and determination to search for the diamonds, and even more work to get them into their most valuable form. Regardless, the diamond miners fare the challenge, and pursue their goal. They endure many obstacles, because they know the value of the end results—fortune! It is their perception that carries them to victory.

Today is the day we take our blinders off. Today we must learn to perceive things as they truly are. Today we know that all things, whether good or bad, will work for our good in the end. Therefore, today we take back our power! We put down the box of Kleenex, gather our strength and get ready to claim our reward. Today we no longer murmur and complain when obstacles come our way. We stand up and ask ourselves the question, "What good can come out of this bad situation?" We stay focused and hold tightly to our road map, which is our organized plan, and we let nothing or no one take us away from achieving our dreams.

Even though you may currently be hurting and struggling to overcome, I challenge you today to turn your tears into praise. You made it another day. You are one day closer to the place where you want to be. There are great things waiting for you just ahead, so dust yourself off and continue on this journey. You're going to make it!

Once you change your perception you can overcome any hurdle in life. You take hold of your power by labeling your experiences. If you label a situation bad, it will become a bad experience. If you label a situation good, you will discover the good in your experience. You alone hold the power of perception! How will you label this journey? However you label it, that will be your experience.

Whatever you do in life, never listen to the "haters," the people who wish you harm. Drown them out. You don't need advice or aid from negative people. The only thing they'll do for you is cause you to sink before you learn how to swim. If you allow people to overshadow you with their perception, you lose the battle before the war starts. Be strong and firm in the confidence that: "This too shall pass. I will learn from this experience and let it go. When I get to the end, there will be a reward for me, because I know all things will work together for my good." When you look at life from this perspective the difficulties that used to knock you down will no longer affect you. The hits that were swung at you, you will no longer feel. You will be armed and focused, ready to conquer the world! You will make it.

Let's take a look at a real-life experience comparable to what many of us are facing now. This example illustrates the power of perception.

Jackie was a nice girl who grew up in a good family in Raleigh, N.C. Her father and mother were both ministers, and Jackie was raised in the church. She earned straight As in school and did everything she was supposed to, until she got to high school. In high school Jackie met new friends, and her whole life began to change. Jackie wanted to be like the "cool kids," so she dropped all the principles her parents taught her and did her best to please her peers. Jackie started skipping school, and her parents began to complain. They were strong disciplinarians, so she was often punished. Jackie got tired of the strict rules in her house and began to rebel. Jackie was introduced by her friend Betty to a drug called heroin. Betty told Jackie this drug would ease her pain and keep her feeling like she was on top of the world. Jackie liked that promise and started abusing heroin. Her addiction started light but quickly picked up. Jackie began stealing from her parents and even the church they attended to get money for her habit. Life at home got worse. Jackie's mother threatened to put her in a group home. Then Jackie ran away.

At fifteen years old, Jackie moved to Las Vegas, Nevada with a fake ID, and she started stripping at nightclubs to feed her habit. Jackie began making lots of money, so she abused drugs even more. Eventually, Jackie was so strung out that she sold her body to keep up her habit. Jackie's life spiraled out of control. She knew deep inside what she was doing was wrong, but she couldn't manage to curb her desire for drugs. Jackie was fed up. She said to herself, "I'm going to turn this last trick and get enough money to go home." She picked up a trick off the strip, and he took her far away from the city. There he beat her badly and robbed her of all the cash she had in her possession. Fearing that the man was going to kill her, Jackie reached in her purse, took out her blade and stabbed the man to death. After her last strike at his neck, she passed out. Jackie woke up the next morning handcuffed to a hospital bed, where she was greeted by Las Vegas Detectives. All she could think was, I'm sixteen years old and my life is over. Jackie began to cry profusely when she found out her victim was dead and that she was being charged with first degree murder. On top of that, the nurse informed Jackie that she was HIV positive. Her blood count was low, so she needed to be treated at the hospital before she could go to jail. Life was over for Jackie, or so she thought. "Why did all these bad things have to happen to me!" she screamed out loud.

Let's take a time out to analyze the events that led to Jackie's incarceration. How do you perceive Jackie's situation? Do you believe any good could come out of this terrible situation? Let's continue reading Jackie's story and find out the answers.

Immediately the police notified Jackie's parents, who had reported their daughter missing. They thought Jackie was abducted. They hadn't seen her in over a year. Jackie's mom began to sob over the phone. She was happy to know her daughter was alive. She told the detectives she and her husband were on their way. Jackie's mom received permission to be by her daughter's side at the hospital where she began to pray. Jackie recommitted her life to God after experiencing her mom's unconditional love. Jackie detoxed in the hospital. She received care for her medical condition, bringing back the vitality and joy that was taken from her by her drug use. Jackie was sad the day her mother had to leave, but it was time for Jackie to go to the county jail. Jackie's mom and dad went back to North Carolina, but Jackie's mom felt depleted. They had a small church with about 50 members whom they loved greatly, but preaching became burdensome for Jackie's parents during such a hard time in their lives. In the county jail, Jackie was able to settle her thoughts, without the influence of drugs. Slowly, she began to come back to life as she ate and took care of herself. One day she got a call to go down for a visit. She wondered who would come to see her all the way in Las Vegas. It was Jackie's parents. They told her that they had turned the church over to one of the associate pastors, and they moved to Las Vegas to be closer to Jackie. All she could do was weep. She realized at that moment how much her parents truly loved her. Three times a week, Jackie's mom and dad would visit her. They always brought their Bibles and instructed Jackie to read and to trust God.

After being in the county jail for a little over two years, Jackie prepared for sentencing. She pled guilty to manslaughter with the stipulation of receiving a 10 year sentence, of which she would have to serve 85%. Jackie's parents had strong faith and believed God would provide a better outcome. In court, Jackie read the letter she wrote to the Judge, asking for mercy. He began to lecture Jackie about her adverse choices and the harm that resulted because of her actions. Jackie was frightened. She just knew the judge was going to throw the book at her. "This is what I'm going to do. I'm going to sentence you to five years imprisonment with 500 hours community service. As a condition of your release, I want you to tell your story to other teens so they won't make the same mistakes you have," the judge ordered as he banged his gavel.

Jackie and her family were overjoyed. By the time Jackie was finally sentenced, she served another year in state prison, and then she was paroled. While Jackie was in prison, her parents opened a new church in Las Vegas, which quickly grew. They ended up with over 1000 members by the time Jackie was released. What a big difference from the small church with 50 members in North Carolina! Jackie came home and became very active in the church. She successfully performed her community service, speaking to hundreds of children in Vegas. During her speaking engagements she met a young man who was also HIV positive and who had given his life to God. Today they are happily married, and like Jackie's parents, they both are ministers. They preach at Jackie's parents' church in Las Vegas. Jackie's testimony and her message of hope is so inspiring that thousands of young people gather at the church each Sunday to have fellowship. To date, the church has over 5000 members who rededicated their lives to God.

What a story! What an ending! Jackie's dilemma ended up becoming her greatest testimony. This can also happen to you, if you look at your current circumstances as a launching pad for your future success. Jackie's parents had been praying for years for their daughter to be saved, and to have a large church where they could minister to many people. Had they not all gone through the trials and tribulations they experienced, they would not be ready for their final destination. It was a test, and they passed! Will you pass your test?

I've seen so many miracles take place in prison. Families have grown closer together. People who were sentenced to life in prison were released. Women who were deemed as "unfixable" got out of prison and opened up companies that made millions of dollars in revenue. These people discovered that they could take their adversity and turn it into an opportunity. They accepted their experience as the gateway to a brighter future. It all started with perception. They had to have the strength to perceive the good that was yet to come. This was only accomplished by their faith. Do you believe good things can happen for you, too?

Today marks your starting point. All that happened in the past is over. All that matters is the present. It's your job to identify what you need to do in this very moment to be the best you can be in life. There are no more barriers in front of you. The power lies in your perception. Will you dare to dream and experience the joy that comes after the rain? Are you ready to receive this joy? If so, let's pray: *"God, I thank You for the mighty miracle of perception. I now understand this experience of imprisonment had to happen. All that I've endured, including the tears, the pain, and the many hardships, will now work out for my good. I ask that You continue to strengthen my faith and lend me Your vision. Allow me to see obstacles as You would perceive them. Give me the unique power of perception to identify the good in every situation. I thank You for all the wisdom and knowledge You have imparted to me. Amen."*

Congratulations! You have arrived. You have all of the weapons and instruments you need to complete this journey. All you have to do is move forward, and never look back!

Let's close this chapter with an affirmation to keep our perception correctly focused at all times: *"Today is a new day. Today I am empowered. I've reached deep down within and have seized the power of perception. I no longer am controlled by what others think and feel. I now possess the power to perceive things as I label them. My experience will be what I pronounce it to be. I will experience joy each and every day, regardless of my circumstances. I will identify the good, even if it is surrounded by darkness. I now possess the ability to overcome every hurdle and every barrier, because I have learned that power lies in my perception. Today, I have arrived. I am indeed successful."*

CHAPTER QUESTIONS

1) What is perception?
2) Why is perception important?
3) How do you change your perception?
4) What happens when we adopt other people's perceptions?
5) How can you utilize the power of perception to overcome hardships?

WRITING ASSIGNMENT

Write down a list of all the challenges you are currently facing. Use your power of perception and forecast what good can come out of these challenges. Then, label your challenges. Give each a new name, which will become your experience, based on your new perception of them.

AFTERWORD

I hope you have enjoyed this journey and are now actively pursuing your dreams. Life wasn't meant to be easy, but you were built to outlast the storm! If you endure the many discomforts that come your way from time to time, you will make it. You now possess the key techniques and strategies to help you overcome. You are not alone. There are many others awaiting your arrival to your destination of purpose. You hold the keys they also need to make it successfully through their journey. They are counting on your success. You now have a Partner who will ensure your greatest victory. Stay focused, and keep your eyes on the prize! You will receive the reward of wholeness, in every aspect of your life.

I would like to remain a part of your success. Please continue on with the next book in the *Voices of Consequences Enrichment Series*, entitled *Pursuit to a Greater "Self."* There's even more for you to learn on this journey.

I've enjoyed our encounter, and I eagerly anticipate many great things to occur in your life.

Don't keep this message to yourself; share it with as many others as you can. Please submit your testimonies to me at:

Voices International Publication Inc.

196-03 Linden Blvd.

St. Albans, NY 11412

If you can, please include a photo of yourself. I would like to share your story with others. I would like to know the lessons you've learned and the wisdom you've gained since reading this book. When you are released from prison, check out my latest updates at www.vocseries.com. I would love to have you be a part of my empowerment coalition.

Congratulations on your success and great blessings.

Love,
Jamila Davis

REFERENCES

CHAPTER ONE

The New King James Version Bible, Nashville, Tennessee: Thomas Nelson Inc., 1982.

Casarjian, Robin. *House of Healing*. Boston: Lionheart Press, 1995.

Meyer, Joyce. *Battlefield of The Mind*. New York: Hachette Book Company USA, 1995.

Warren, Rick. *The Purpose Driven Life*. Zondervan, 2002.

Williamson, Marianne. A *Return to Love*. New York: Harper Collins Publishers, 1992.

CHAPTER TWO

The New King James Version Bible, Nashville, Tennessee: Thomas Nelson Inc., 1982.

Meyer, Joyce. *Battlefield of The Mind*. New York: Hachette Book Company USA, 1995.

Peale, Norman Vincent. *The Power of Positive Thinking*. Prentice Hall, 1996.

CHAPTER THREE

Allen, James. *As A Man Thinketh*. Raddord, VA: Wilder Publications, 2007.

Byrne, Rhonda. *The Secret*. New York: Atria Books, 2006.

The New King James Version Bible, Nashville, Tennessee: Thomas Nelson Inc., 1982.

Jordan, Bernard. *The Laws of Thinking*. Hay House, 2006.
Meyer, Joyce. *Battlefield of The Mind*. New York: Hachette
Book Company USA, 1995.
Peale, Norman Vincent. *The Power of Positive Thinking*.
Prentice Hall, 1996.
Williamson, Marianne. *A Return to Love*. New York: Harper
Collins Publishers, 1992.

CHAPTER FOUR

The New King James Version Bible, Nashville, Tennessee:
Thomas Nelson Inc., 1982.
Warren, Rick. *The Purpose Driven Life*. Zondervan, 2002.

CHAPTER FIVE

Canfield, Jack. Hansen, Mark and Hewitt, Les. *The Power
of Focus*. Deerfield Beach Florida: Peale, Health
Communications Inc., 2000.
Hill, Napoleon. *Think and Grow Rich*. Capstone, 2009.

CHAPTER SIX

Canfield, Jack. Hansen, Mark and Hewitt, Les. *The Power
of Focus*. Deerfield Beach Florida: Peale, Health
Communications Inc., 2000
Hill, Napoleon. *Think and Grow Rich*. Capstone, 2009.

CHAPTER SEVEN

The New King James Version Bible, Nashville, Tennessee:
Thomas Nelson Inc., 1982.
Byrne, Rhonda. *The Secret*. New York: Atria Books, 2006.
Hill, Napoleon. *Think and Grow Rich*. Capstone, 2009.
Jordan, Bernard. *The Laws of Thinking*. Hay House, 2006.

Meyer, Joyce. *Battlefield of The Mind*. New York: Hachette Book Company USA, 1995.

Peale, Norman. Vincent. *The Power of Positive Thinking*. Prentice Hall, 1996.

Warren, Rick. *The Purpose Driven Life*. Zondervan, 2002.

CHAPTER EIGHT

The New King James Version Bible, Nashville, Tennessee: Thomas Nelson Inc., 1982.

Hill, Napoleon. *Think and Grow Rich*. Capstone, 2009.

Simmons, Russell. *Do You*. New York: Gotham Books, 2007.

CHAPTER NINE

Allen, James. *As A Man Thinketh*, Raddord, VA: Wilder Publications, 2007.

Byrne, Rhonda. *The Secret*. New York: Atria Books, 2006.

The New King James Version Bible, Nashville, Tennessee: Thomas Nelson Inc, 1982.

Hill, Napoleon. *Think and Grow Rich*. Capstone, 2009.

Peale, Norman Vincent, *The Power of Positive Thinking*. Prentice Hall, 1996.

Simmons, Russell. *Do You*. New York: Gotham Books, 2007.

CHAPTER TEN

The New King James Version Bible, Nashville, Tennessee: Thomas Nelson Inc, 1982.

Canfield, Jack. Hansen, Mark and Hewitt, Les. *The Power of Focus*. Deerfield Beach Florida: Peale, Health Communications Inc., 2006.

Warren, Rick. *The Purpose Driven Life*. Zondervan, 2002.

CHAPTER ELEVEN

Canfield, Jack. Hansen, Mark and Hewitt, Les. *The Power of Focus*. Deerfield Beach Florida: Peale, Health Communications Inc., 2006.

Hill, Napoleon. *Think and Grow Rich*. Capstone, 2009.

CHAPTER TWELVE

The New King James Version Bible, Nashville, Tennessee: Thomas Nelson Inc., 1982.

Byrne, Rhonda. *The Secret*. New York: Atria Books, 2006.

Jordan, Bernard. *The Laws of Thinking*. Hay House, 2006.

Peale, Norman Vincent. *The Power of Positive Thinking*. Prentice Hall, 1996.

Williamson, Marianne. *A Return to Love*. New York: Harper Collins Publishers, 1992.

About the Author

Jamila T. Davis, born and raised in Jamaica Queens, New York, is a motivational speaker and the creator of the Voices of Consequences Enrichment Series for incarcerated women. Through her powerful delivery, Davis illustrates the real-life lessons and consequences that result from poor choices. She also provides the techniques and strategies that she personally has utilized to dethrone negative thinking patterns, achieve emotional healing, and restoration and growth.

Davis is no stranger to triumphs and defeats. By the age of 25, she utilized her business savvy and street smarts to rise to the top of her field, becoming a lead go-to-person in the Hip-Hop Music Industry and a self-made millionaire through real estate investments. Davis lived a care-free lavish lifestyle, surrounded by rap stars, professional sports figures and other well known celebrities.

All seemed well until the thorn of materialism clouded Davis' judgments and her business shortcuts backfired, causing her self-made empire to crumble. Davis was convicted of bank fraud, for her role in a multi-million dollar bank fraud scheme, and sentenced to 12 1/2 years in federal prison.

Davis' life was in a great shambles as she faced the obstacle of imprisonment. While living in a prison cell, stripped of all her worldly possessions, and abandoned by most of her peers, she was forced to deal with the root of her dilemmas- her own inner self.

Davis searched passionately for answers and strategies to heal and regain her self-confidence, and to discover her life's purpose. She utilized her formal training from Lincoln University, in Philadelphia, Pennsylvania, along with her real-life post-incarceration experiences and documented her discoveries. Revealing the tools, techniques and strategies she used to heal, Davis composed a series of books geared to empower women. Davis' goal is to utilize her life experiences to uplift, inspire and empower her audience to achieve spiritual and emotional wholeness and become their very best, despite their dilemmas and past obstacles.

Voices International Publications Presents

Voices of CONSEQUENCES
ENRICHMENT SERIES
CREATED BY: JAMILA T. DAVIS

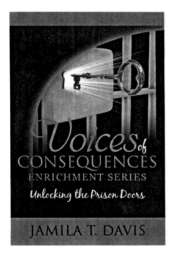

Unlocking the Prison Doors: 12 Points to Inner Healing and Restoration

ISBN: 978-09855807-4-2 Textbook
ISBN: 978-09855807-5-9 Workbook/Journal
ISBN: 978-09855807-6-6 Curriculum Guide

Unlocking the Prison Doors is a nondenominational, faith-based instructional manual created to help incarcerated women gain inner healing and restoration. In a comforting voice that readers can recognize and understand, this book provides the tools women need to get past the stage of denial and honestly assess their past behavioral patterns, their criminal conduct and its impact on their lives and others. It provides a platform for women to begin a journey of self-discovery, allowing them to assess the root of their problems and dilemmas and learn how to overcome them.

This book reveals real-life examples and concrete strategies that inspire women to release anger, fear, shame and guilt and embrace a new world of opportunities.

After reading *Unlocking the Prison Doors,* readers will be empowered to release the inner shackles and chains that have been holding them bound and begin to soar in life!

INTERNATIONAL PUBLICATIONS
"Changing Lives One Page At A Time."
www.vocseries.com

Voices International Publications Presents

$\mathcal{V}oices_{of}$
CONSEQUENCES
ENRICHMENT SERIES
CREATED BY: JAMILA T. DAVIS

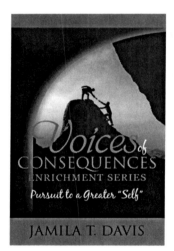

Pursuit to A Greater "Self:" 12 Points to Developing Good Character and HealthyRelationships

ISBN: 978-09855807-7-3 Textbook
ISBN: 978-09855807-8-0 Workbook/Journal
ISBN: 978-09855807-9-7 Curriculum Guide

Pursuit to A Greater "Self" is a non-denominational, faith-based, instruction manual created to help incarcerated women develop good character traits and cultivate healthy relationships.

This book is filled with real-life examples that illustrate how good character traits have helped many people live a more prosperous life, and how deficient character has caused others to fail. These striking examples, along with self-help strategies revealed in this book, are sure to inspire women to dethrone bad character traits and develop inner love, joy, peace, patience, kindness, generosity, faithfulness, gentleness and self-control. This book also instructs women how to utilize these positive character traits to cultivate healthy relationships.

After reading *Pursuit to A Greater "Self,"* readers will be inspired to let their light shine for the world to see that true reformation is attainable, even after imprisonment!

"Changing Lives One Page At A Time."
www.vocseries.com

"Every negative choice we make in life comes with a consequence. Sometimes the costs we are forced to pay are severe!"
— Jamila T. Davis

She's All Caught Up is a real-life cautionary tale that exemplifies the powerful negative influences that affect today's youth and the consequences that arise from poor choices.

Young Jamila grew up in a loving middle class home, raised by two hardworking parents, the Davises, in the suburbs of Jamaica Queens, New York. Determined to afford their children the luxuries that they themselves never had, the Davises provided their children with a good life, hoping to guarantee their children's success.

At first it seemed as though their formula worked. Young Jamila maintained straight As and became her parents ideal "star child," as she graced the stage of Lincoln Center's Avery Fischer Hall in dance recitals and toured the country in a leading role in an off-Broadway play. All was copacetic in the Davis household until high school years when Jamila met her first love Craig- a 16 year old drug dealer from the Southside housing projects of Jamaica Queens.

As this high school teen rebels, breaking loose from her parents' tight reins, the Davises wage an "all-out" battle to save their only daughter whom they love so desperately. But Jamila is in too deep! Poisoned by the thorn of materialism, she lusts after independence, power and notoriety, and she chooses life in the fast lane to claim them.

When this good girl goes bad, it seems there is no turning back! Follow author, Jamila T. Davis (creator of the Voices of Consequences Enrichment Series) in her trailblazing memoir, *She's All Caught Up!*

AUGUST 2013
ISBN: 978-09855807-3-5
www.voicesbooks.com

INTERNATIONAL PUBLICATIONS

ORDER FORM

Mail to: 196-03 Linden Blvd.
St. Albans, NY 11412
or visit us on the web @
www.vocseries.com

QTY	Title	Price
	Unlocking the Prison Doors	14.95
	Unlocking the Prison Doors Workbook/Journal	14.95
	Permission to Dream	14.95
	Permission to Dream Workbook/Journal	14.95
	Pursuit to A Greater "Self"	14.95
	Pursuit to A Greater "Self" Workbook/Journal	14.95
	Total For Books	
	20% Inmate Discount -	
	Shipping/Handling +	
	Total Cost	

* Shipping/Handling 1-3 books 4.95
          4-9 books 8.95
* Incarcerated individuals receive a 20% discount on each book purchase.
* Forms of Accepted Payments: Certified Checks, Institutional Checks and Money Orders.
* Bulk rates are available upon requests for orders of 10 books or more.
* Curriculum Guides are available for group sessions.
* All mail-in orders take 5-7 business days to be delivered. For prison orders, please
allow up to (3) three weeks for delivery.

SHIP TO:

Name: _____

Address: _____

_____

_____

City: _____

State: _____ Zip: _____

CPSIA information can be obtained at www.ICGtesting.com
Printed in the USA
BVOW01s1534240913

331929BV00007B/107/P

9 780985 580742